# KAMALA DAS AND HER POETRY

*Second Revised and Enlarged Edition*

A.N. Dwivedi

PUBLISHERS & DISTRIBUTORS (P) LTD

Published by

**ATLANTIC**

**PUBLISHERS & DISTRIBUTORS (P) LTD**

7/22, Ansari Road, Darya Ganj, New Delhi-110002
Phones : +91-11-40775252, 40775214, 23273880, 23275880
Fax: +91-11-23285873
Web: www.atlanticbooks.com
E-mail: orders@atlanticbooks.com


Second Revised & Enlarged Edition, 2000

Reprint 2006, 2009, 2011, 2020, 2023



Printed & bound in India by Atlantic Print Services

**DEDICATED TO**

**PROF. M.K. NAIK**

for his passionate devotion to scholarship

# Preface to the Second Edition

The second edition of this book is being brought out on the persistent demand of the academic community. The book remained out of print for quite some time. In its present edition, it has been thoroughly revised and enlarged. A new Appendix-B has been added to it on Kamala Das's prose works in order to enable the reader to have a composite picture of this author.

I am grateful to Dr. K.R. Gupta, Managing Director, of M/s Atlantic Publishers and Distributors, New Delhi for accepting the book for publication in its present format.

**A.N. Dwivedi**

# Preface to the First Edition

The post-Independence Indo-English verse has gained in both strength and variety in an appreciable manner owing to the salutary efforts of its skilled practitioners. Indo-English fiction that had earlier earned recognition and acceptability is now being supplemented by this indigenous verse, thanks to the talent and craftsmanship of Nissim Ezekiel, Kamala Das, Dom Moraes, A.K. Ramanujan, Pritish Nandy, Shiv K. Kumar, R. Parthasarathy, Jayanta Mahapatra, K.N. Daruwalla, Keshav Malik and a few others. The stature of Kamala Das among these 'new' Indo English poets may be judged from the fact that she has been included in all the important anthologies and special issues of various journals and magazines the world over. She also finds a place on the syllabi of several Indian and foreign universities. And she comes next to none in points of popularity and recognition as a poet.

Although Kamala Das has produced only three slender volumes of verse to-date, she stands out as an Indian poet writing in English today by virtue of her lyricism, openness and frankness. In her case, quality steals a march over quantity. There are so many Indo-English poets with a number of volumes to their credit, but they do not possess the quality of Kamala Das. One gram of gold is certainly more valuable than one kilogram of copper. One has to tread very cautiously in the field of contemporary Indo-English verse.

Kamala Das is verily a celebrant of the human body, and her poetry is glutted with images and symbols of love and lust. Her exemplary candour and sincerity of tone renders her verse highly readable and enjoyable, and one simply can't stop without reaching unto the very last. What adds pungency and authenticity to it is the distillation of her own experiences into it, the recording of her personal concerns and predicaments in it. There is a strong autobiographical touch in it, which makes Mrs. Das a 'confessional' poet of the first order — somewhere near Anne Sexton, Sylvia Plath and Judith Wright among women poets and Theodore Roethke, Robert Lowell, W.O. Snodgrass and John Berryman among men poets. As a true 'confessional' poet, she 'hides nothing' from her readers (to borrow a phrase from Anne Sexton), including what is ugly and forbidden.

Kamala Das has already attracted, a good deal of notice from scholars and critics in the academic world. There are already book-length studies on her, such as those of Devinder Kohli and Anisur Rahman, but a fresh appraisal of her poetic work and worth is always called for. Moreover, I am fully aware of the salient features as well as the shortcomings of both the books, and to do away with the latter I have taken up this project in great earnest. While Kohli's makes useful preliminary investigations into the poetic tools and techniques of Kamala Das, relying heavily on a close chronological scrutiny, Rahman's is severely restricted in its compass due to its doctoral character. Without minimizing the importance of these two works, the present one makes a comprehensive survey of Mrs. Das's poetical collections and endeavours to project her in a proper perspective. In addition, it critically examines her novel, *Alphabet of Lust* (1976), in an Appendix towards the close of the book, and in so doing it becomes the first of its kind.

In writing this book, I have incurred the obligations of some institutions and libraries, especially of the members of the Library staff of the universities of Allahabad and Bombay, and I wish to register my sense of appreciation of their efficiency and promptness.

**A.N. Dwivedi**

# Contents

# 1

# Kamala Das: A Biographical Sketch

Kamala Das, who looms large over the poetic horizon of today's India, hails from the South, precisely from the Southern Malabar in Kerala, where her grandmother, Nayar father and Nalapat mother used to live peacefully beside the fathomless sea. She was born (March 31, 1934) and bred here, and received her education, for the most part, at home. Why her parents who were poets themselves of a certain taste and stature adopted this attitude towards her education is not known. As her autobiography tells us, Kamala Das whose maiden name was Madhavikutty first attended a European school in Calcutta, then the Elementary School at Punnayurkulam (which is her birth-place), and then a boarding school run by the Roman Catholic nuns, but in each of them she stayed for a short while. At the Catholic boarding school, she got ill and was removed to Calcutta where private tutors were engaged to teach her fine arts.

Her father, who had married in 1928, belonged to a traditional family having an aristocratic atmosphere around it. Though this family was not financially well-off, her father had been employed in an automobile firm in Calcutta, where he sold Rolls Royces, Humbers and Bentleys to the Indian princes and their relatives. Speaking of her parents' unsuited alliance, Kamala writes: "My mother did not fall in love with my father. They were dissimilar and horribly mismated."[1] But her mother's timidity created an illusion of domestic harmony, and produced some half a dozen children of swarthy skin and ordinary features.

Kamala's parental home was influenced by the movement of Mahatma Gandhi, and its members used to wear *khadi* clothes and even spin *khadi* yam, especially her grandmother, to whom this girl was deeply attached in her early age and whom she remembered so sweetly in her

[1] Kamala Das, *My Story* (New Delhi: Sterling Publishers, 1976), p. 5.

later life. Mahatma's photos hung in every room. Even the servants felt his presence in the house and began wearing *khaddar.* The Nalapat House — that is how her ancestral home was called — consisted of seven occupants in all, who were her grandmother, her aunt Ammini, her grand uncle, the poet, her great grandmother, her two sisters, and Mahatmaji.

At the age of 15, Kamala Das was married to Mr. Das, an official in the Reserve Bank of India, Bombay, where her life became miserable in the company of her nonchalant, lustful husband. As he was experienced in sex with his maidservants, his contact with his wife was usually cruel and bmtal. He boasted to have known of 'sluts and nymphomaniacs', and this prompted Kamala to launch into 'a hectic love life with small capital — just a pair of beautiful breasts and a faint musk-rat smell in my perspiration....' She grew revengeful towards him, and reacted in a non-traditional fashion in love-making, offering herself to any handsome or resourceful man who came across her, and forgiving even her rapists. Her husband had no soothing words for her, no time to spare for her and was ever busy sorting out his files and affixing his signature on them. And as a traditional wife, she was expected to discharge her domestic duties well and to look to the needs and comforts of her husband. This eroded her own distinct personality and dwarfed her for ever, as she makes clear in the poem "The Old Playhouse":

> ...You called me wife,
> I was taught to break saccarine into your tea and
> To offer at the right moment the vitamins. Cowering
> Beneath your monstrous ego I ate the magic loaf and
> Became a dwarf. I lost my will and reason, to all your
> Questions I mumbled incoherent replies.

This is actually a strong protest against a hollow marital bond which she cannot untie. In India where marriage and love go hand in hand, it is most unfortunate that such a sensitive woman as Kamala Das is tied to a stake whence she cannot fly (to use a Shakespearean expression). Such occurrences are not uncommon in the land of Gandhi and Nehru, turning many a woman tragic and gloomy in their attitude towards life. Kamala Das has made repeated protests against this sort of situation in her poetry.

But the woman-poet continues to live with her husband and look after her three children (all sons). When she speaks of love outside marriage, she does not really advocate for infidelity and adultery, but merely searches for a kind of man-woman relationship which should guarantee both love and security to a woman. And it is important to note that she gives a mythical framework to her search for genuine love and identifies it with the Radha-Krishna myth or with the Mira-Krishna relationship. There are several poems on Lord Krishna in her volumes, supported by references to this Lord in her prose writings (especially in *My Story* and *Alphabet of Lust).*

Kamala Das who has lived long in such metropolitan cities as Bombay, Calcutta, and Delhi, and who has written a lot about them, is now settled in Trivandrum, Kerala. She writes in both Malayalam and English, and has published eleven books in her mother tongue and three books of poems in English. Her poetical collections in English are: *Summer in Calcutta* (1965), *The Descendants* (1967), and *The Old Playhouse and Other Poems* (1973). She has collaborated with Pritish Nandy in *Tonight, This Savage Rite* (1979), a collection of their love poems. Her *autobiography, My Story,* which was first serialized in The Current Weekly of Bombay from January to December, 1974, has now come out as an independent work (1976). She has also published a novel in English under the title, *Alphabet of Lust* (1976).

For Kamala Das, the period between 1968 and 1973 seems to have been less poetic and more prosaic. Her prose written after *The Descendants* is almost exclusively autobiographical. "Frigidity and the Sepia-tainted Photograph" clearly deals with her personal experiences and with the subject of love and emotional discontentment in an empty married life. Though her prose writings are controversial, her essays like "I Studied All Men," "What Women Expect Out of Marriage and What They Get," "Why Not More Than One Husband?" and "I Have Lived Beautifully" tend to consolidate her image in public as feminine yet forthright, unconventional yet honest, ebullient yet tragic, impetuous yet insecure, — an image also projected by her poems in three volumes.

Besides her poetical and prose works, Kamala has written extensively for various popular magazines and periodicals, such as *Opinion, The Illustrated Weekly of India, Poetry East and West, Debonair, Eve's Weekly, Femina, Imprint, Weekly Round Table, and Love and Friendship.* In the beginning of her career, she used to write short stories in Malayalam for *Mathrubhumi*, a magazine which paid her rupees 12 per story, and her poems for *The Illustrated Weekly*, whose editor, Mr. Mandy, was very considerate towards her and used to explain reasons for his inability to publish anything. How feverishly she wrote then may be gathered from her well-known autobiography:

> I typed nearly a thousand words a week. I wrote about the subjects the editors asked me to write on, fully aware that I was uneducated

> by the usual standards and that I had no business meddling in grave matters. But how happily I meddled to satisfy that particular brand of readers who liked me and liked my honest approach. I was useless as a housewife anyway. I could not pick up a teapot without gasping for breath. But writing was possible.
>
> And it certainly brought me happiness.[2]

That she could write even during her illness is quite evident from this extract.

In the end, Kamala Das is the only woman poet of India writing in English today who has attained worldwide recognition. She has been given a prominent place in all the leading anthologies of Indo-English poetry, nay of Commonwealth poetry. She was offered the P.E.N.'s Asian Poetry Prize in 1963, and the Kerala Sahitya Academy Award in 1969 for her *Thanuppu*, meaning *Cold*, a collection of short stories in Malayalam.

2. *My Story*, p. 218.

# 2

# The Body of Das's Poetry

Kamala Das's poetry is concerned with both the external and internal worlds, and her response to the external world in particular, despite her inner restlessness, is marked by an admirable sense of poise and perfection. While Pritish Nandy's poem about Calcutta ("Calcutta if you must exile me") is an ambitious poem evoking a landscape at once frenzied and explosive, Mrs. Das's outer landscape, though part of the inner landscape, can still retain its objective contours. Nandy dwells on an aspect of life in Calcutta and seems to be rhetorical, but Kamala Das lets the details speak for themselves before they speak for her.

### I. Summer in Calcutta (1965)

This poetical work opens with the poem "The Dance of the Eunuchs," which sets the tone (of irony) and temper of the entire volume. There are many poems on the theme of love, but few which speak of the glory belonging to a really exalting love-experience. "The Dance of the Eunuchs" objectifies, through an external, familiar situation, the poet's strangled desire within. It was written against the background of the poet's sudden contact with 'a man who had hurt me when I was fourteen years old;' she wanted 'to get him at any cost.' The poem is powerful and bold indeed, and displays an admirable sense of proportion in the use of imagery and metaphor.

The next poem, "The Freaks," paints a rather helpless situation when the man is passive and the woman is burning with desire, but she is helpless. It is about 'a grand, flamboyant lust.' Another poem, "In Love," brings the poet face to face with the question whether she could call her sexual experience 'love.' It is aglow with heat and passion. "In Winter" also carries the warmth of the sexual act, of her soul 'groping for roots' in his body. "A Relationship", too, identifies love with physical desire. — 'It was my desire that made him male/And beautiful.' The poem "Spoiling the Name" mocks at the significance generally attached to words and, figuratively, to abstractions. A name is an abstraction, and in a woman's case borrowed from someone else; it is a weight and a burden, as all abstractions are. She, therefore, asks:

> ...why should this name, so
> Sweet-sounding, enter at all the room
> Where I go to meet a man
> Who gives me nothing but himself, who
> Calls me in his private hours
> By no name....

This poem shows Mrs. Das's craftsmanship, but is rhetorical in tone.

"An Apology to Goutama" constructs a dialectical opposition between the ascetic and the sensual, between Goutama and her own man. The opposition is actually between two kinds of eyes, two kinds of voices, two kinds of faces, rather two modes of living:

> ...while your arms hold
> My woman-form, his hurting arms
> Hold my very soul.

The poem rests on this vital contrast for its strength.

"The Fear of the Year" highlights a gloomy mood. "My Grandmother's House" has also the mood of 'wild despair':

> ...I who have lost
> My way and beg now at a stranger's doors to
> Receive love, at least in small change?

And in "The Wild Bougainvillea" we hear about the poet's sadness and how she 'groaned/And moaned, and constantly yearned for a man from/ Another town....' In "The End of Spring," the poet, while waiting for her lover's phone call, sinks into brooding over 'the fear of change.' And "Too Early the Autumn Sights" also evokes a mood of premature desiccation within:

> Too early the autumn sights
> Have come, too soon my lips
> Have lost their hunger, too soon
> The singing birds have
> Left.

Even in this poem of so conventional a mood, Mrs. Das is able to squeeze out of common images a bit of visionary quality.

"Visitors to the City" is a passionate etching of a scene composed of 'sights and sounds' offered by one morning on Strand Road.

"Punishment in Kindergarten" is warm and muffled, and recounts the picnic of the poetess at Victoria Gardens to which she and her classmates were taken, and the incident which followed it (as Kamala Das tells us in her autobiography). She was all alone near the hedge, while other girls were playing at a distance. The poem demonstrates the poet's capacity to smell the flowers as well as the pain of being slighted. It has hardly any suggested larger meaning.

The title-piece, "Summer in Calcutta," projects, through action and gesture, a self-contained mood of sensuous luxury. The image of the April sun in it brings to the poet a sense of sensuous repletion, of warm intoxication which inspires as well as relaxes so that 'my worries doze' and

> ...wee bubbles ring
> My glass, like a bride's
> Nervous smile, and meet
> My lips. Dear, forgive
> This moment's lull in
> Wanting you, the blur
> In memory.

The poem celebrates the mood of temporary triumph over 'the defeat of love.' It is an Indian poet's creative reaction to the torture of the Indian summer. What distinguishes Kamala Das's reaction is her unconscious intimacy with this torture.

"The Siesta" is associated with sleep, 'the sun-lit tank,' which brings 'an anonymous peace' to her, or with dreams which 'glow pearl-white.' But what the mysterious siesta brings to her is neutralized by her supposed inability to meet 'this alien world which talks/Of Gods and casual sins.' However, the poet is concerned more with the vulnerability of 'the anonymous peace' of the siesta, its inability to withstand the challenge of the wakeful world rather than with the siesta itself. The display of the potency of this challenge is the poet's oblique commitment to it.

"With Its Quiet Tongue" expresses the poet's agonised concern with the wretched coldness of heart. Another poem, "My Morning Tree" deals with the familiar theme of desperate longing for fulfilment. Its images are sharp, structure is carefully organized, and mood poignantly objectified. In it the poet looks forward to the moment of the blossoming of 'a sudden flower,' though the images like the 'ugly tree' and the 'fleshless limbs' of the tree give no hope of this blossoming. The poem is one of dark despair; and the sense of fulfilment which so strongly dominates poems such as "Winter," "A Phone Call in the Morning," "Love," "Spoiling the Name," "In

Love," is here imagined and telescoped but not without involving the cost of an almost brutal irony, for the blossoming may not only come too late but may be the end itself. The 'passive' limbs of her desires and passion will flower into a 'red, red morning flower' of death.

"The Testing of the Sirens" is a befitting close to the book looking backwards as far as "The Dance of the Eunuchs." The poet wakes up from a night full of love and lust to a sense of physical loneliness, goes through a drive with another man with 'a pock-marked face' and, while he is taking her photograph, arises with a keen desire for love which is doomed to remain unfulfilled. Her relationship with either of lovers is a rootless and detached loyalty of the moment, to the first (of the night) that of the limbs and to the second (with the 'pock-marked face') that of 'a smile' which is 'such a detached thing.' The poem immortalises the poet's attachment to one of her family friends, a young man of eighteen years, who used to take her out to Victoria Memorial, photographing her against trees and against flowing water, and entertaining her with Hindi film songs.

In *Summer in Calcutta*, we have a different category of poems like "The Flag," "Someone Else's Song," "Forest Fire," "An Introduction," and "The Wild Bougainvillea," in which there is an attempt to rise above the 'private voice' and depict a larger panorama of experience. The technique is almost always one of assuming a vaster identity (as in Whitman or Tagore), as in "Someone Else's Song":

> I am a million, million people
> Talking all at once, with voices
> Raised in clamour, like maids
> At village-wells.

Or, in "The Stranger and I":

> I've seen you in restaurant, all gay
> And smoke-filled, on the seat behind
> The pillar, drinking joylessly your
> Sweetened tea, while your left hand
> Softly trembling, crouches on the
> Tablecloth like a wounded bird....

Despite the fact that the majority of poems in the volume are dominated by a tone of betrayal and present the poet as a prisoner of her own loneliness and complex moods, the poem "The Wild Bougainvillea" satisfies a peculiarly personal need as a necessary distraction from her mood of sadness and loneliness: 'It is good world, and packed with distractions.' The poem "An Introduction" is a candid and witty piece of self-revelation, and is a beautiful statement of her poetic credo, her attitude to language and experience. 'Fit in,' said they. 'Belong,' cried the categorizers. But the burden of the poem, as indeed of Mrs. Das's entire work, is to have the freedom to be herself, it is to be herself. Here she transforms her alienation from 'critics, friends, visiting cousins,' who say, 'Don't write in English,' into a larger and more universal alienation (sexual, social and artistic):

> ...I met a man, loved him. Call
> Him not by any name, he is every man
> Who wants a woman, just as I am every
> Woman who seeks love.

It is, however, clear from a large number of poems in *Summer in Calcutta* that Kamala Das's impersonal note or sense of universality is simply self-imposed and not natural for her. In this volume, the personal moods and feelings triumph over the impersonal ones, for sustained universality is not within the poet's reach.

### II. The Descendants (1967)

This second poetical volume by Kamala Das has twenty-three poems in all. Most of these poems are further variations of her favourite theme of sexual love. This collection is, by and large, bitterly death-conscious, perhaps death-obsessed. And some of these poems like "The Descendants," "The Invitation," and "Composition" look to be sobered by compassion or humility under a false impression. The truth is that there lurks beneath the pseudo-metaphysical poise the inability to reckon with emotional defeat and frustration, with a sense of nothingness[1]:

> To be frank,
> I have failed.
> I feel my age and my Uselessness.
> ("Composition").

The poetess is actually overwhelmed by the smouldering 'secret' that 'I am so alone,' and that life is a colourless design of crumbling patterns, as in the poem "A Request":

> When I die
> Do not throw the meat and bones away
> But pile them up
> And

1. Devinder Kohli, *Virgin Whiteness: The Poetry of Kamala Das* (1968), p. 18.

Let them tell
By their smell
What life was worth
On this earth
What love was worth
In the end.

The 'meaninglessness' of the poetess's life is sourly conveyed in the above-given passage, as also in such poems as "Shut Out That Moon" and "Neutral Tones." The negation of all positives in life reminds us of Thomas Hardy.

The title poem, "The Descendants," borders on nihilism which moves the poet in a direction opposite to the faith in the essential continuity of life suggested by "Death Brings No Loss" (*Summer in Calcutta*). This poem concludes with a ring of finality: 'We are not going to be/Ever redeemed, or made new.'

Another poem, "The Suicide," has weak passages and lacks a dramatic cohesion. It is constructed as a conversation between the poet and the sea. The theme is the poet's contemplated or suggested suicide, but the poem finally rejects it through a renewal of the sense of life. As in her view the body and the soul are inseparable, the poet can't choose between a physical death and a spiritual death. For her, the sea is the source of a constant distraction, a nagging threat, and invites her to negation:

The sea is garrulous today. Come in,
Come in. What do you lose by dying, and
Besides, your losses are my gains.

It offers her dissolution in a seductive way.

The strains of death so explicit in "A Request" run through 'Dear night, be my tomb' of "Substitute" and merge into the unredeemed darkness of our fate, of the wounds and the cross, of the fire and 'the hungry earth' of "The Descendants" which would devour us in the end.

In "The Invitation," while the sea offers one kind of death, a complete negation, her lover whom she can't disobey offers another, metaphorical death — the feeling of 'lying on a funeral pyre/With a burning head.' The language of delirium suggests the feeling of torture that seems to accompany her more recent treatment of sexual love. In this poem, the poet rejects the way of the sea and prefers to shrink or grow in her own way. Although the man has gone for good, the poet is warmed by the memory of her experience. She can't forget the self-contained intensity of the moment of sexual love:

All through that summer's afternoons we lay
On beds, our limbs inert, cells expanding

Into throbbing suns. The heat had
Blotted our thoughts....

There is a suffusing organic warmth in these lines.

The poem "Ferns" arrests sexual love in an image of self-devouring and self-mocking intensity which suggests that perhaps there is a sense in which her glorification of physical love carries with it an element of disenchantment. Another poem, "Convicts," depicts physical love in the elemental terms of physical labour and heat, and as a physical experience which belongs to no intellectual language:

That was the only kind of love,
This hacking each other's parts
Like convicts hacking, breaking clods
At noon. We were earth under hot
Sun. There was a burning in our
Veins and the cool mountain nights did
Nothing to lessen heat. When he
And I were one, we were neither
Male nor female.

This is a very sensuous poetic passage indeed.

"Substitute" is both poignant and truculent. The need to conform to the conventions of a hypocritical society makes one's feeling of emptiness all the more painful. The poem is poignant, and is ironical in its meditative refrain:

It will be all right if I join clubs
And flirt a little over telephone.
It will be all right, it will be all right
I am the type that endures.
It will be all right, it will be all right
It will be all right between the world and me.

The abrupt intrusion of the image of crows over the market square flailing the sky 'with raucous cries' breaks the spell of this refrain only to prepare the ground for the suggestion of the lack of 'mental contact' between the man and the woman in "Our bodies after love-making/ Tumed away, rejecting." The tone of the poem is Prufrockian. The pursuit of love in it is merely mechanical without any meaning.

Another poem concentrating on sexual love is "The Looking Glass":

...Notice the perfection
Of his limbs...
...All the fond details that make

Him male and your only man. Gift him all,
Gift him what makes you woman, the scent of
Long hair, the musk of sweat between the breasts,
The warm shock of menstrual blood, and all your
Endless female hungers.

It is both patronising and indulgent in tone.

The poem "Captive" describes Kamala Das's love as 'an empty gift,' 'a gilded empty container' and herself as the prisoner of 'the womb's blinded hunger, the muted whisper at the core.' The poem is ambiguous in tone, but the theme of sexual love receives greater relevance from the glory of creation, of childbirth. The same theme finds expression also in her "Jaisurya," which combines the narrative and the meditative, and which details the whole gamut of feelings preceding and following the birth of a son. It brings together light and darkness, fire and water, to weave a pattern of feeling which holds itself up with the joy of creation. It is significant that meaningful things happen to the poetess at or around noon time under the virgin whiteness of the sun. The child is a day that is 'Separated from darkness that was mine/And in me.'

The newly bom child is set against the background of 'war', 'bloodshed and despair' in "The White Flowers". The simple prayer wishing her son a long life in the face of the outer threat of violence and death is strengthened by the contrast between the white flowers (standing for peace, long life) and the red (standing for blood, mortality, anarchy) of the cherry wine, the rose. The solitary gesture of heroism is traceable in —

Today some of us will rise and sing of love
In voices never as sweet before, for love like life
Is sweetest just before its end.

But the glasses are 'cold like a dead man's palm' and there is the horror and the ghastly wailing which tends to subdue the poet's prayer for the preservation of the child.

### III. The Old Playhouse and Other Poems (1973)

This collection of poems came out in 1973, and contains 33 poems in all. Of these, fourteen are old poems taken from *Summer in Calcutta* and six from *The Descendants*. The poems reprinted from *Summer in Calcutta* are: "The Freaks," "In Love," "Love," "*Summer in Calcutta*," "An Introduction," "The Wild Bougainvillea," "My Grandmother's House," "Forest Fire," "A Relationship," "The Snobs," "Corridors," "Loud Posters," "I Shall Some Day," and "Drama," and those from *The Descendants* are:

"Composition," "The Suicide," "Luminol," "Convicts," "Palam," and "The Descendants." Thus, the collection has only thirteen new poems to be considered here.

The title-piece, "The Old Playhouse," tells us that love is perhaps no more than a way of learning about one's self or the completion of one's own personality. It is addressed presumably to the husband, and is largely personal. It lodges a protest against the constraint of the married life: the fever of domesticity, the routine of lust, artificial comfort, and male domination. 'You' in the poem is possibly the husband, who wants to tame the swallow who is the woman and thus deprive her of her natural freedom. As a result of his egotism, she feels emptied of all her natural mirth and clarity of thinking:

> ...You called
> me wife,
> I was taught to break saccarine into your tea and
> To offer at the right moment the vitamins. Cowering
> Beneath your monstrous ego I ate the magic loaf and
> Became a dwarf. I lost my will and reason, to all your
> Questions I mumbled incoherent replies.

Here the woman suggestively protests against the male ego and assertion.

A different kind of protest — against the fanaticism of — religion is obvious in "The Inheritance." This poem is bitter, ironical, but not cynical. It deals with the hatred and intolerance that goes in the name of religion, whether it is Islam, Christianity, or Hinduism. What man has inherited is not love but hatred, not wisdom but babble: 'this ancient/ Virus that we nurtured in the soul....'

"Blood" is the only new poem in the longer genre like "Composition" and "The Suicide." Here the onrush of emotions is admirably restrained. It is largely autobiographical, and the poetess's nostalgia for the old house and for the great grandmother who lived in it is convincingly evoked. Mrs. Das does not idealize the house and the people associated with it; she also does not attempt to reach out into the history of the house of three hundred years beyond what she herself knows of it. Presently, it is an old house with the walls 'cracked and tom and moistened by the rains,' and with the fallen tiles, the whining windows and the rats scampering past the door. The grandmother, who is 'really simple,' 'fed of God for years,' and proud of her 'oldest blood,' is portrayed with humour and detachment. More than the pathos of the memory of her grandmother, the poem is concerned with the poet's sense of death and decay. Its short and crisp lines indicate a solemnity of tone and a gravity of mood. Even where Kamala Das speaks of defeat and emptiness and the inevitable darkness which is imminent, the assured clarity of outline, the serious control of nerve, and the poise of movement confirm that the poet is in command of herself in a moment of personal reminiscence. There is a pervasive sense of death and decay in the following lines:

> I know the rats are running now
> Across the darkened halls
> They do not fear the dead
> I know the white ants have reached my house
> And have raised on walls
> Strange totems of burial.
> At night, in stillness,
> From every town I live in
> I hear the rattle of its death
> The noise of rafters creaking
> And the windows' whine.
> I have let you down
> Old house, I seek forgiveness.

Here memory is mixed with sadness.

The poem "Nani" is a peculiar blend of irreverence and gravity. The pregnant maid, 'the dark plump one, who bathed me near the well,' and who hanged herself in the privy, seemed —

> A clumsy puppet, and when the wind blew
> Turning gently on the rope, the seemed
> To us who were children then, that Nani
> Was doing, to delight us, a comic
> Dance....

Time moves on and the incident is forgotten by the grandmother, but not by the poet. The poem ends abruptly with the poet admiring the 'clotted peace' of the dead. Perhaps the poet identifies herself with the dead, but paradoxically the imagery which evokes the peace of the dead belongs not to the world of the dead but to that of the living world.

"Gino" starts on a note of warning and fear, comparing the kiss of a lover to the bite of a krait who 'fills the bloodstream with its accursed essence.' This makes her think of the all pervasive essence of love, and of the sense of death which is also the sense of life:

> ...a July, full of rain, and darkness
> Trapped like smoke, in the hollows of the sky, and
> That lewd, steamy smell of rot, rising out of the earth.

There is a conflict between. the desire to experiencthis poisonous love, possibly love outside marriage, and the difficulty to 'dislodge the inherited memory of a touch.' But if this difficulty is anyhow overcome, thoughts of the triumphant love haunt the poet and she dreams of 'obscure hands/ Striding up my limbs,' of ward boys, sepulchral, wheeling me through long corridors/To the x-ray room's dark interior,' of 'aeroplanes! Bursting red in the sky,' of 'fat/Half-caste children, lovelier than Gods,' and of 'Drinking wine in verandahs.' And in a sudden transition of thought, she realises that her dreams are unreal and that the burden of the body growing uncomely and gross is more real:

> This body that I wear without joy, owned
> By man of substance, shall perhaps wither, battling with
> My darling's impersonal lust. Or, it shall grow grass
> And reach large proportions before its end.

The poet is obviously articulating here her sense of disease, death and decay of everything beautiful.

The poem "Glass" focuses the attention on the fragility of love-experience ('half an hour') and also of the body. The poet says with a sense of pathos:

> I went to him for half an hour
> As pure woman, pure misery
> Fragile glass, breaking
> Crumbling

In contrast to this self-hurting womanliness, the lover

> ...drew me to him
> Rudely
> With a lover's haste, an armful
> Of splinters, designed to hurt, and,
> Pregnant with pain.

In this poem, the restlessness of the poet is voiced through a Freudian search for the misplaced father-figure. She moves from man to man in search of her true home, but there is a sense of wasted effort in the prolonged search. And what in poems such as "Vrindavan," "Radha-Krishna," and "Lines Addressed to a Devadasi" is mythologized as the woman's search for Krishna, the eternal lover, is given in "Glass" a clinical version as an attempt 'to look for him the "misplaced" father now everywhere.'

In "The Prisoner," the poetess compares herself to the convict who 'studies his prison's geography' with distrust and hope:

I study the trappings
Of your body, dear love,
For I must some day find
An escape from its snare.

The term 'trapping' is very significant, for it suggests "the trappings of lust from which she must free herself to know true love" as well as "the soul's cry against its mortal dress."[2] Usually the convict attempts to escape from the prison only to return to his normal course of life. What Mrs. Das suggests here is the fact that there is no real freedom from imprisonment of this world or of lust.

"The Stone Age," like "The Old Playhouse," deals with the reality of love being offered to the poetess by another man rather than by her husband. This poem portrays the husband of the woman-persona as 'old fat spider' who weaves 'webs of bewilderment' around her and erects the dead, dull stony wall of domesticity, comfort, lassitude, and thus turning her into 'a bird of stone, a granite dove.' The husband is the perpetual irritant, an unwelcome intruder into the privacy of the wife's mind, which is haunted by other men. When the husband goes out, she drives along the sea and climbs 'the forty noisy steps to knock at another's door.' Now the act of defiance having taken place, the deed done, freedom asserted, and the dull cocoon of domesticity assaulted, the lines suddenly come alive with the energy of questioning:

...Ask me, everybody, ask me
What he sees in me, ask me why he is called a lion,
A libertine, ask me the flavour of his
Mouth, ask me why his hand sways like a hooded snake
Before it clasps my pubis. Ask me why like
A great tree, filled, he stumps against my breasts,
And sleeps. Ask me why life is short and love is Shorter still, ask me
what is bliss and what its price....

The freedom that we come across in these lines is the kind of freedom the poetess longs for.

"After the Illness" was written after the poetess's recovery from a protracted illness. It is concerned with the theme of survival of herself as well as of the lover's love for her. It was 'perhaps the deeply hidden soul' that kept his love intact.

The ambiguity of the image of 'bed-room mirrors' which occurred in "Gino" is more fully exploited in "The Motif in the Mirror." The

2. D. Kohli, *Kamala Das* (1975), p. 113.

ambiguity of the image of visual density lies in its being invested with a symbolic mobility. The sense of sensuous repletion is conveyed in this poem not merely by this visual density, this repetition of motif in a visual picture, but also suggested by the image of circular movement in water of swimming in pools. The elusiveness of love is expressed in 'this reflection of a reflection, this shadow of a shadow, this dream of a dream.'

"The Millionaires at Marine Drive" is both astringent and meditative in nature, its subject being the incurable loneliness of the woman. The warmth which her grandmother gave her still haunts the poetess because no man has been able to give her such a genuine love. The grandmother is presented here as an embodiment of tenderness and warmth, and contrasted with her:

> ...all the hands
> The great brown thieving hands groped beneath my
> Clothes, their fire was that of an arsonist's,
> Warmth was not their aim, they burnt my cities
> Down....

There was, in fact, never any 'mental contact' between herself and her husband. What she wanted was a lovable 'identity' with him, but her circumstances brought her only the pain of growing old with 'a freedom I never once had asked for.' This poem makes a shift in Kamala Das's approach to love-theme, and from the glorification of sexual love she now moves to a general dissatisfaction with the male character which tries to dwarf the woman in her.

# 3

# Main Themes of Das's Poetry

Kamala Das moves in a narrow range in her poetry. Like Jane Austen in English fiction, her range of themes is limited. Very often there is witnessed repetition, and consequent monotony, in the body of her poetical works. However, she moves in her circle with grace and skill. She does not try to transgress her self-imposed limitations, and this accounts for her success in poetical endeavours. In fact, broad political, financial, and social issues were beyond her reach, but whatever she wrote was born of her own experiences which immediately make her an integral poet, a poet of felt thought.

Kamala is primarily a poet of feminine longings. Her poetry and prose reflect her restlessness as a sensitive woman moving in the male-dominated society, and in them she appears as a champion of woman's cause. She raises her forceful voice against the male tyrannies in such poems as "A Relationship," "*Summer in Calcutta*," "An Introduction," and "Marine Drive," and in such essays as "Why Not More Than One Husband?" and "What Women Expect Out of Marriage and What They Get." In them she comes out as an ardent spokesman (or, spokeswoman) of women's 'lib' movement. Kamala expresses the secret hopes and fears of womankind as seen in the poem "Afterwards":

> Son of my womb,
> Ugly in loneliness.
> You walk the world's bleary eye
> Like a grit. Your cleverness
> Shall not be your doom
> As ours was.

(*Summer in Calcutta*, p. 55).

The above-quoted lines highlight a mother's concerns for her son. And the following poetic passage reveals the monotony and tiresomeness of a hollow married life:

I shall someday leave, leave the cocoon
You built around me with morning tea,
Love-words flung from doorways and of course
Your tired lust. I shall someday take
Wings, fly around...

(*Summer in Calcutta*, p. 52).

Evidently, Kamala speaks here as a 'liberated' woman, who resents 'the cocoon' built around her and desires to flit about without any restrictions. The fairer sex receives a better deal from this sensitive poetess, who airs out its grievances and sufferings in a striking fashion.

Mrs. Das is unquestionably a poet of love and sex. As such, she is not so much preoccupied with the metaphysical quest of a restless soul, nor with the formulation of any theory of poetry. She writes almost invariably about the power of love and the appeal of the body. She confesses that she "...wrote the poems in the book *Summer in Calcutta* to make a man love me, to break down his resistance."[1] As an honest poet of love, she looks very frank and naive, without the 'intellectual pride' and the domestic air of the well-known Australian poetess, Judith Wright. It should, however, be remembered that Kamala Das wrote her poetry against a more conservative and tabooed society than that of Wright. She has, therefore, more to say about the pathos of a woman emerging from a passive role to the point of discovering and asserting her individual liberty and identity. More often than not she concentrates on sexual love, and her woman-persona rises as though in a mood of revolt. The love poems of Kamala usually breathe an air of unconventionality and urgency. Mark the following extract in this connection:

Of late I have begun to feel a hunger
To take in with greed, like a forest-fire that
Consumes, and, with each killing gains a wilder,
Brighter charm, all that comes my way.
...My eyes lick at you like flames, my nerves
Consume; and, when I finish with you, in the
Pram, near the tree and, on the park bench, I spit
Out small heaps of ash, nothing else.

("Forest Fire," *Summer in Calcutta*, p. 51)

and again:

A man is a season,
You are eternity.

---

1. Cited from D. Kohli's *Kamala Das*, p. 29.

To teach me this, you let me toss my youth like coins
Into various hands, you let me mate with shadows,
You let me sing in empty shrines, you let your wife
Seek ecstacy in others' arms...

..................................................

...Perhaps I lost my way, perhaps
I went astray. How would a blind wife trace her lost
Husband, how would a deaf wife hear her husband call?
("A Man is a Season," *Tonight, This Savage Rite*, p. 21).

It would be, in truth, no exaggeration to say chat love is the *leitmotif* of Kamala's poetry through and through.

Related to the theme of love is the theme of the body in Mrs. Das's verse. Sometimes she likes her body, while at others she dislikes it. Physically, she is 'dark' with ordinary features, and her loathing for the body is mainly due to this factor as well as to her protracted illness. In liking the body, she resembles Nissim Ezekiel, who is also a 'poet of the body.' Both these poets, like American 'Confessional' poets, accept wholeheartedly the demands of the body. As for Kamala Das, the tensions of the body issue forth in her poetry from a pressure of her complex family background — she was not properly cared for during her childhood nor well attended to in her married life. And as she says in her essay "I Have Lived Beautifully,"[2] her marriage was doomed to fail right from the beginning: "My husband was immersed in his office-work, and after work there was the dinner, followed by sex. Where was there any time left for him to want to see the sea or the dark buffaloes of the slopes?" Possibly, the failure of love is linked with the birth of poetry and its fulfilment in case of Kamala Das. The following is a fine piece of poetry written with the sole purpose of celebrating the body, reminding us of Walt Whitman in modem American poetry:

Yes,
It was my desire that made him male
And beautiful, so that when at last we met
To believe that once I knew not his
Form, his quiet touch, or the blind kindness
Of his lips was hard indeed. Betray me?

.........................................................

Yes, he can, but never physically
My body's wisdom tells and tells again

[2] *Debonair,* III, No. 5 (May 15, 1975), 41.

That I shall find my rest, my sleep, my place
And even death nowhere else but here in
My betrayer's arms....

("A Relationship").

And here is the poem "A Request" depicting the hatred of the poetess for the body:

When I die
Do not throw
The meat and bones away
But pile them up
And let them tell
By their smell
What life was worth
On this earth
What love was worth
In the end.

The latter piece shows that she is fed up with the present way of her life and that she is pricked deep down within without a ray of hope for redemption.

Kamala Das's poetry contains an acute concern for decay and death. Her autobiography, bordering on fiction occasionally, was actually written during one of her serious illnesses. It is not that she is afraid of death, and the last portions of *My Story* tell us that she was sometimes even ready to welcome it, but physical decay and destruction definitely haunt her inescapably. The poem "Lines to a Husband" has two parallel strands in it — obsession with decay and death and obsession with love (which could not be had at the legitimate source). The simultaneous pull of these obsessions renders the poetess hopeless and helpless, and in deep anguish she cries out:

From the debris of house wrecks
Pick up my broken face,
Your bride's face,
Changed a little with the years.
I shall not remember
The betrayed honeymoon;
We are both such cynics,
You and I.

In her *My Story*, Kamala tells us that she, at the age of 19, suffered a nervous breakdown as a 'neglected wife,' and that she was commanded to live all alone in a closed room with sunshine peeping through a window. She fell seriously ill and was removed to Malabar, where her grandmother's affectionate care could cure her. Of all persons, Kamala liked her grandmother best whose house was 'a paradise on earth for me.' In the poem "My Grandmother's House," she remembers this house as a source of great comfort abounding in love for her:

> There is a house now far away where once
> I received love...that woman died,
> The house withdrew into silence, snakes moved
> Among books I was then too young
> To read, and, my blood turned cold like the moon.
> How often I think of going
> There.... (*Summer in Calcutta*, p. 15).

No doubt, one of the loved central characters in Kamala's work is her great grandmother who is usually associated with her memory of the parental home in Malabar now more than three hundred years old but tinged with regality. The poem "Blood" is actually an apotheosis of this home — 'this old house beside the sea,' and the poetess's fascination with the images of the house beside the sea can clearly be traced back to her childhood associations with it.

Mrs. Das is a poet not so much of the countryside as of the city. In this context, she is utterly contrasted to such poets as K.N. Daruwalla who are so alive to the sights and sounds and colours of idyllic countryside. In fact, Kamala deplores her moving away from a beautiful atmosphere beside the seashore surrounding her parental house to the 'dusty cities' with their hustle-bustle. Another noted poetess, Gauri Deshpande, rightly points out a general lacuna in contemporary Indo-English verse — the absence of the countryside details and events — in her Foreword to *An Anthology of Indo-English Poetry*, and Kamala is no exception to this. And if we look for her strength as a poet, we must detect in her poetry the dust, the heat, the crowds, the poverty of India combined with the misery and endurance of womankind. She has actually seen too much of the city, its commotion and horrors and dens of vices, to be 'idyllic' about anything else. The 'city' is an integral part of her existence and she can't shake off its impressions and memories easily. She rather tries to strike a sort of synthesis between the changing reality of a private passion and the apparently unchanging reality of the shining sun on Indian horizon. In this connection, the overtones of the poem "Summer in Calcutta" in the first volume must be taken into account. It is a synthesis which is almost spontaneous and unconscious in its compulsive drive. Kamala Das uses neither the biting social irony of Nissim Ezekiel, nor the larger philosophical themes of Sri Aurobindo or even of Tagore, but she is not totally alienated from the Indian landscape or its social milieu like our well-known expatriates Dom Moraes and Tilottama Rajan.

Kamala's being a typical poet of the city is quite evident from her persistent use of the metaphor of the city for life, such as in the poem "A New City":

I have come with only a picnic bag
To this new city,
To seek a blind date, to shed as snakes do,
In coils and coils, my Weariness.

(*Summer in Calcutta*, p. 38).

Nissim Ezekiel also is with Kamala Das in expressing his sense of annui and boredom toward the city of Bombay — 'The city wakes, where fame is cheap,/And he belongs an active fool' ("A Morning Walk"). But in Ezekiel the sense of loss is of a different nature; it is 'depersonalized,' so to say. On the contrary, Kamala *feels acutely* for the loss of her parental home and pure love by making the city as her 'new' home. Coupled with this anguished awareness of her loss is her eloquent expression of the pleasures and charms to be found in a big city. She discovered 'all the Delhi streets...fragrant murky,' and here she became once more 'young, very lovely and delightfully carefree'. Elsewhere she contrasts the impressive tranquillity of the Delhi landscape with the disturbed state of her mind. The one city which told heavily on her nerves is Bombay, and yet she bids a touching farewell to it in one of her moving poems:

I take leave of you, fair city, while tears
Hide somewhere in my adult eyes
And sadness is silent as a stone
In the river's unmoving
Core....
It's goodbye, goodbye, goodbye,
To slender shapes behind windowpanes
Shut against indiscriminate desire
And rain....

("Farewell to Bombay," *Summer in Calcutta*, p. 39).

A separation from anything is ever painful, and the intellectual oneness that Kamala might have experienced in this grand city makes her say a tearful goodbye to it.

Finally, Kamala Das is a poet of moods and freaks, and hence she writes about so many other things 'that momentarily arrest her attention; *e.g.*, about pigeons, seasons, children, bangles, the sea-shore and the morning tree, bats, phone calls, artificial alarums, airports, the ferns and the maggots, the joss-sticks and the looking-glasses, convicts, problems of composition, the high tides and the loud posters, the swamp and the blue bird. These various things have been catalogued here in order to show that Kamala Das does emerge from her well-chosen themes now and then, and thereby create an impression of diversity and variety. She is as felicitous in their handling as in that of her familiar themes. And together, they create the impression on the reader's mind that her poetry is "as honest, it is as human, as she is."[3] The narrowness of her range is thus widened and the monotony caused by frequent reversions to the same subject and mood partly removed.

3. Sophia Wadia, "Foreword", *Summer in Calcutta* (New Delhi: Everest Press, 1965), p. 7.

# 4

# As a Poet of Love and Sex

Kamala's concerns as a poet are not philosophical or mystical or spiritual; they are also not directed towards the propagation of a commitment or the formulation of a theory of poetry. More than to these, she is dedicated to the celebration of love in all its aspects. In the act of this celebration, she may not love the robustness and the democratic temper of Walt Whitman, nor the intellectual stamina of the 'Confessional' poets like Anne Sexton, Robert Lowell, Theodore Roethke, Sylvia Plath, and Judith Wright, but she has in her the most essential qualification to do so — the richness of emotions, the profuseness of deep feelings. The very nature of her verse reflects her emotional temper, which makes her feel ill at ease with the present-day materialistic world trying to lay a siege around her.

Added to this is her personal predicament. During her childhood, Kamala, like other children in the Nair family, was almost completely neglected but for her grandmother. This is what she tells us in her popular autobiography:

> He [her father] was not of an affectionate nature. So we grew up more or less neglected, and because we were aware of ourselves as neglected children in a social circle that pampered the young, there developed between us a strong relationship of love, the kind a leper may feel for his mate who pushed him on a hand-cart when they went on their begging rounds.[1]

And when at the early age of fifteen, she was married to an insensitive and unsympathetic man, her pathos in life deepened with no streak of regeneration. Her prose writings, including *My Story*, tell us repeatedly that her marriage floundered on the rocks of ruin right from the start. Her husband, who devoted all his time to the official files, had no leisure

1. *My Story*, p. 2.

to spare for his sensitive bride who used to hanker for a fulfilment in love, for an emotional attachment. No doubt, he had earned for her security and money, but that alone could not satisfy an extraordinarily gifted woman. Writing of her husband, she says:

> My husband was immersed in his office-work, and after work there was the dinner, followed by sex. Where was there any time left for him to want to see the sea or the dark buffaloes of the slopes?[2]

To live in such a cramping atmosphere is neither desirable nor healthy. Consequently, Kamala feels frequently like a helpless bird put in a cage — 'I'm tied to a stake; I cannot fly' (to borrow a Shakespearean expression). This goes a long way in turning her vision tragic and her verse melancholy.

In Kamala's three volumes of verse, there are a number of poems that breathe an air of love, amorousness, and sexuality. But these should not lead one to believe that she has been pleading all along for promiscuity and adultery. They rather articulate her strong desire to get liberated from the clutches of a male-dominated society and pass a happy, healthy life of peace and rest. The woman-persona in her asserts an 'indomitable will' and 'the spirit of revenge' (to use Milton's popular phrases), and gives a clarion-call to the weaker sex to rise in revolt against all kinds of repression and tyranny being perpetrated on it. Kamala as a poet is never tired of speaking aloud for womankind as a whole, and several of her poems should be read in this light.

Having cleared the position of Kamala Das as a poet of love and sex — which is hardly ever conventional or conservative, it is pertinent to have a look at the vast corpus of her love poetry. Beyond a shadow of doubt, love/sex occupies a prominent place in her poetry and emerges as one of its dominant themes.

*Summer in Calcutta* has a fairly good number of poems on love and sex. Such poems are: "The Freaks," "In Love," "My Grandmother's House," "A Relationship," "Loud Posters," "Love," "The Bangles," "The Sea Shore," "*Summer in Calcutta*," "The Sun Shine Cat," "Forest Fire," "Afterwards," and "The Testing of the Sirens." Of these poems, some are about the poetess's pure love for a near and dear one, while many others are about her disillusionment in love, and only a few about lust. The poems "My Grandmother's House," "Love," "Afterwards," etc. are of the first category, while "The Freaks." "A Relationship," "Loud Posters," "The Bangles," "The Sea Shore," etc. are of the second, and "In Love," "*Summer in Calcutta*," and "Forest Fire" are of the third. There are different shades of love in Kamala's poetry, and the very first volume bears ample evidence of it. In "Love," she expresses her happiness and contentment in love:

2. "I Have Lived Beautifully", Debonair, III, No. 5 (May 15, 1975), 41.

Until I found you,
I wrote verse, drew pictures,
And, went out with friends
For walks....
Now that I love you,
Curled like an old mongrel
My life lies, content,
In you....

(*Summer in Calcutta*, p. 31).

This poem is, clearly without any pricks, without any tensions. There is no craving for the lips meant for others, no instinct of challenge, no streak of complaint, as one usually finds in love poetry. But this kind of mood is only short-lived for Kamala, and she soon swings back to her usual grudge and grouse against men (who might have harmed or teased her). She might even accept the inevitable married life for a girl and its responsibilities, but not without lodging her forceful complaint against malekind as a whole and hollow marital relationships. This is how we discover her saying in "A Relationship":

Yes,
It was my desire that made him male
And beautiful, so that when at last we
Met, to believe that once I knew not his
Form, his quiet touch, or the blind kindness
Of his lips was hard indeed. *Betray me?*
*Yes, he can, but never physically*;
Only with words .......................
.......................................... while,
My body's wisdom tells and tells again
That I shall find my rest, my sleep, my peace
And even death nowhere else but here in
My betrayer's arms ....

(*Summer in Calcutta*, p. 18) (*Italics mine*).

Obviously, she does not like 'physical' love that her strong husband showers on her; she rather craves for emotional identity which he fails to afford for her. And here is the hot, though somewhat unwilling chase of the inordinate desire of passion:

Of what does the burning mouth
Of sun, burning in today's
Sky remind me...oh, yes, his

Mouth, and...his limbs like pale and
Carnivorous plants reaching
Out for me, and the sad lie
Of my unending lust.

(*Summer in Calcutta*, p. 14).

If 'burning' marks this hot chase here, her 'hunger' for sex appears clearly in the poem "Forest Fire." The first few opening lines are given below for an illustration:

Of late I have begun to feel a hunger
To take in with greed, like a forest-fire that
Consumes, with each killing gains a wilder,
Brighter charm, all that comes my way.

(*Summer in Calcutta*, p. 51).

This 'hunger' is intemperate and terrible in nature as its simile with the wild 'forest-fire' signifies. The discontent in love at the legitimate source is definitely responsible for this condition of hers, and through the poet-persona the whole Hindu social set-up comes in for a sharp criticism. In this rotten set-up, marriages are made without taking into account the suitability of the partners from various angles — their family background, age, education, financial status, and social connections. Kamala Das raises her voice of resentment against this hollow set-up.

The story of personal anguish and dilemma in love continues in the next two volumes of Kamala — The *Descendants* and *The Old Playhouse and Other Poems*. Several poems in these volumes are written in the same mood and tone as witnessed in the first. The poetess returns to the theme of love and sex repeatedly with all urgency and sincerity. Many of the poems are suffused with warmth and passion, with heat of an unrequited love and an unfulfilled desire. The frequency of the love theme may evoke repudiation from nuns and spinsters and breed boredom in the minds of general readers, but like Sappho in Greek literature, like Elizabeth Barrett Browning in English letters, and like Anne Sexton and Sylvia Plath in modem American poetry, Mrs. Das offers us a feast of vivid images of love couched in felicitous language. No doubt, love is her *forte* in poetry.

In *The Descendants*, we have such poetic pieces on the subject of love and lust as "A Request," "Substitute," "The Descendants," "Ferns," "The Invitation," "Captive," "The Proud One," "The Conflagration," "The Looking Glass" and "Convicts." In this poetical collection the fury of the poetess at not receiving adequate love from the proper person deepens into the debunking irony and tragic vision of a pitiable nature. There is no laughter, no humour in it, and Kamala's pessimism touches a hellish depth. Poem after poem she hammers hard at her husband-lover and articulates her intense desire of escaping from his clutches and attaining 'freedom.' This is what we have in the poem "Substitute":

> Yet, I was thinking, lying beside him,
> That I loved, and was much loved.
> It is physical thing, he said suddenly,
> End it, I cried, end it, and let us be free.
> This freedom was our last strange toy.

(*The Descendants*, p. 7).

But this 'freedom' does not give her 'pride,' nor 'joy,' nor a sense of security, nor a name, and in great dejection she tells us:

> After that love became a swivel-door,
> When one went out, another came in.

The 'right' kind of man she wanted has never met her. This is at the core of her tragedy:

> For long I've waited for the right one
> To come, the bright one, the right one to live
> In the blue. No. I am still young
> And I need that man for construction and
> Destruction. Leave me....

("The Invitation", *The Descendants*, p. 14)

and again:

> what have
> we had, after all, between us but the
> womb's blinded hunger, the muted whisper
> at the core... For years I have run from one
> gossamer lane to another, I am
> now my own captive.

("Captive", *The Descendants*, p. 17).

The kisses of her husband on her cheeks are the 'maggots' rolling over 'the corpse' (p. 22). He knows only the 'physical' kind of love, without trying to make any emotional or spiritual contact with her. This idea is neatly expressed in the poem "Convicts":

> That was the only kind of love,
> This hacking at each other's parts
> Like convicts hacking, breaking clods
> At noon. We were earth under hot

Sun. There was a burning in our
Veins and the cool mountain nights did
Nothing to lessen heat.

(*The Descendants*, p. 26).

This kind of love is bound to degenerate and drift lovers apart who feel the necessity of getting relieved by some other sources. The poem "The Joss-Sticks at Cadell Road" elaborates this inherent idea:

My husband said, I think I shall
Have a beer, it's hot,
Very hot today.
And I thought, I must
Drive fast to town and
Lie near my friend for an hour. I
Badly need some rest.

(*The Descendants*, p. 23).

That the couple will go two different ways for the sake of removing boredom and dissatisfaction is quite evident in this passage. The noted Indo-English poet, R. Parthasarathy, has rightly observed in this connection — "The despair is infectious. Few of her poems have, in fact, escaped it."[3] Possibly one of the 'boiling' love poems in this volume is "The Looking Glass," wherein the poetess offers us details of the secret of a true love-making. She says herein:

Getting a man to love you is easy
Only be honest about your wants as
Woman. Stand nude before the glass with him
So that he sees himself the stronger one
And believes it so, and you so much more
Softer, younger, lovelier...Admit your
Admiration. Notice the perfection
Of his limbs, his eyes reddening under
Shower, the shy walk across the bathroom floor,
Dropping towels, and the jerky way he
Urinates. All the fond details that make
Him male and your only man.

and further:

Gift him all,
Gift him what makes you woman, the scent of
Long hair, the musk of sweat between the breasts,
The warm shock of menstrual blood, and all your

3. *Ten Twentieth-Century Indian Poets*, p. 22.

Endless female hungers. Oh yes, getting
A man to love is easy, but living
without him afterward may have to be
Faced.

(*The Descendants*, p. 25).

This sort of 'openness and frankness' is hardly to be found in any other Indo-English woman poet. The resultant emerging picture is a man or a woman of flesh and blood, a living biological reality, with no distortions or twists. Naturally, Kamala is at her best here as a poet of love and sex.

The third volume, *The Old Playhouse...*, has also a few charming poems of love and lust in it. They are: "The Old Playhouse," "Glass," "The Prisoner," "The Corridors," "The Stone Age," and "Sunset, Blue Bird." The title-piece lodges a strong protest against the instinct of possessiveness incarnate in the poetess's husband:

You planned to tame a swallow, to hold her
In the long summer of your love so that she would forget
Not the raw seasons alone, and the homes left behind, but
Also her nature, the urge to fly, and the endless
Pathways of the sky.

Here the husband stands all for suppression and cruelty, while she wishes 'to fly,' to attain freedom. As a proud husband conscious of his glittering gem called 'wife,' he has totally annihilated her identity and individuality. She is treated as no more than a domesticated woman who is required to look after his house and children and attend to his whims and freaks. She is aware of this fact, and complains:

You called me wife,
I was taught to break saccharine into your tea and
To offer at the right moment the vitamins. Cowering
Beneath your monstrous ego I ate the magic loaf and
*Became a dwarf.* I lost my will and reason, to all your
Questions I mumbled incoherent replies. The summer
Begins to fall.

(*The Old Playhouse and Other Poems*, p. 1)
(*Italics mine*).

She reverts to the complaint again and again, and in the poem "The Stone Age" she utters aloud thus:

Fond husband, ancient settler in the mind,
Old fat spider, weaving webs of bewilderment,
Be kind. You turn me into a bird of stone, a granite
Dove....

(*The Old Playhouse and Other Poems*, p. 51).

Her helplessness is complete here, and she urges her unfeeling husband to 'be kind' to her and not treat her as a mere object of pleasure and lifelessness. In another poem, "The Swamp," she calls him "the richest the strongest the deadliest" (p. 53). The closing piece of the volume highlights the shattering of her dreams, the battering of her high hopes — "he no longer calls for me he no longer comes to me or stands at the open window to smile at me..." (p. 54). The poems "The Prisoner" and "The Corridors" are also written in the same vein and style, but the stings are not so severe and tortuous.

It would be not irrelevant to mention here two books in particular — the first is *Tonight, This Savage Rite* (1979) and *An Anthology of Indo-English Love Poetry* (1976). The first one contains the love poems of Kamala Das and Pritish Nandy (who is also an outstanding Indo-English poet of today). Mrs. Das is represented by 34 poems in it (as against 41 pieces by Nandy). The second book is of a different nature and deals with the love poems of a number of poets, both old and new. It is edited by Subhas C. Saha, who includes only 6 of Das's poems. Of these poems, two are put under the sub-heading "Agony Despair Loneliness" — "Autumn Leaves" and "Sunset, Blue Bird;" two under "Union Marriage Children" and are known as "A Losing Battle" and "A Request;" and one under "Other Than Conjugal Love" and is titled "Ghanshyam." While one can say nothing about the propriety of Saha's selection, one can definitely question his exclusion of Kamala Das from the sub-heading "Sensuousness Sensuality" (just as one can do so with regard to his inclusion of Aru Dutt's "Morning Serenade," which is not her own but a translation of Victor Hugo's original poem in French).

There is yet another aspect of Kamala Das's love poetry which has not been touched hitherto, and it is the mythical framework given to her quest for true love. This mythical framework is identified with the Radha-Krishna syndrome, or occasionally with the Mira Bai-Krishna relationship. It is this framework that saves her, in some degree, from the charges of obscenity and promiscuity, otherwise her poetry is replete with shocking and unorthodox details about love and marriage and sex. Though no one can absolve her totally from the charge of sensuality, she tries in certain poems to rise above the sexual mud clinging to her image. The Radha-Krishna syndrome is continually associated with the progress of the poet and is witnessed in all her poetical collections. The first one contains "Radha-Krishna;" the second one has "Radha;" the third one mentions "prayers to unfamiliar Gods" (p. 50); and *Tonight, This Savage Rite* includes "Radha" and "Ghanashyam." Apparently Kamala is pricked by an inner urge to rise above the mere earthly and give vent to her mystical longing or purity and nobility. She has undoubtedly a soul within her body and she can't ignore its calls completely. Indirectly, she believes that the defiling of the body has nothing to do with the resplendent and wakeful soul. In the poem "The Suicide," the poet is evidently concerned with this problem, and says:

> Bereft of soul
> my body shall be bare.
> Bereft of body
> my soul shall be bare.
> ....................................
> I throw the bodies out,
> I cannot stand their smell.
> Only the souls may enter
> The vortex of the sea.
> Only the souls know how to sing
> At the vortex of the sea.

(*The Descendants*, p. 1).

On getting fed up with the physical and the carnal, the poet takes resort to the Radha-Krishna type of love:

> This becomes from this hour
> Our river and this old Kadamba
> Tree, ours alone, for our homeless
> Souls to return someday
> To hang like bats from its pure
> Physicality....

("Radha-Krishna," *Summer in Calcutta*, p. 37).

In another poem of identical character, "Radha," she says:

> The long waiting
> Had made their bond so chaste, ..........
> ......................................................
> And virgin crying
> Everything in me
> Is melting, even the hardness at the core
> O Krishna, I am melting, melting, melting
> Nothing remains but

You ..........

(*The Descendants*, p. 9).

She raises her head from stupor and slumber, goes out in search of her true love, and discovers Krishna or Ghanashyam as her trusted lover. This is forcefully articulated in the poem "Ghanashyam":

Ghanashyam,
You have like a koel built your
Nest in the arbour of my heart
My life, until now a sleeping jungle
Is at last astir with music.

(*Tonight, This Savage Rite*, p. 18).

In an illuminating article, "The Road to Brindavan: The Theme of Love in Kamala Das's Poetry," M.L. Sharma has dwelt at length on this aspect of pure love in the poetry of Kamala Das, but Sharma grows a little zealous in his attempt to vindicate the position of the poetess. One must remember that she has invited adverse opinions, and to some extent reasonably so, from several critics with regard to her frequent reversion to the subject of physical love. Interpretations may vary, but the hardcore reality will not change. Notice what Sharma says about her: "Throughout the chequered career of her loves and lusts, it is Lord Krishna who has been her true paramour and her quest is always single-minded; directed towards Him...."[4] This is certainly not true on the whole. Though there are references[5] in *My Story* to substantiate what Sharma says, one should not accept them as altruisms.

In the end, Kamala Das is a delightful poet of love and sex, unravelling the mysteries of the finer sex in this matter. The 'openness' and the 'honesty' that we find in her is rarely witnessed in other Indo-English women poets, with the possible exception of Gauri Deshpande in a lesser degree. In fact, many others contemporary Indian poets have sung songs in honour of Love — such poets as Shiv K. Kumar, Pritish Nandy, Nissim Ezekiel, R. Parthasarathy, Jayanta Mahapatra, and A.K. Ramanujan — but in her emotional sweep and lyrical rapture Kamala Das surpasses them all. Love is the citadel where her personal cares and anxieties, her own dilemmas and predicaments, are safely anchored.

4. M.L. Sharma in *Contemporary Indo-English Verse*, ed. Dwivedi, p. 108.
5. See the autobiography, pp. 92, 95, 109, 113-14, 179, 190-91, 195, 196-97, etc.

# 5

# As a 'Confessional' Poet

Kamala Das, who is a 'confessional' poet, writes in the mode and pattern of several 'new' American poets like Robert Lowell, Anne Sexton, Sylvia Plath, W.D. Snodgrass, John Berryman, and Theodore Roethke. To all these American poets the critic M.L. Rosenthal gave the adjective 'confessional.' All these poets are highly subjective and write with considerable frankness and sincerity. They usually focus the reader's attention on 'the trials of life, their misery and heartache, often at the sacrifice of beauty for its own sake.' The three outstanding books written in this mode are: Lowell's *Life Studies* (1959), Snodgrass's *Heart's Needle* (1967), and Roethke's *The Lost Son* (1948). Of these, Lowell's book exerted the most profound influence upon the other poets in the genre. It is not suggested here that Kamala imitated the above-mentioned American poets in composing her poetry, but that by reasons of identical subjects and their treatment and strong subjectivism she, too, writes like them.

Before we start tracing features of 'confessional' poetry in the works of Kamala Das, it would be proper to pause for a while here and take stock of this *genre* as a whole. All 'confessional' poetry springs from the need to 'confess,' and so each poem cast in this mode is in some way, according to Robert Phillips, "a declaration of dependence," or of guilt, ox of anguish and sufferings[1]. A 'confessional' poet places no barriers between his self and direct expression of that self, as T.S. Eliot and Ezra Pound used to do. As contrasted to Eliot's and Pound's impregnable 'objectivity,' one finds deep subjectivism, even to the point of irritation, in him. The 'confessional' poet does not accept restrictions on subject-matter, though they are usually personal. He may write as freely about his hernia as about his sweet-heart. Anything within his private experience may form

1. Robert Phillips, *The Confessional Poets* (1973), p. 8.

his theme. He takes the help of an open language for an uninhibited expression of his emotions, and by 'open language' is meant free verse or blank verse, as opposed to rhymed verse (which is so much restricted). It does not suggest, however, that the 'confessional' poets are wild in their emotional outbursts. Furthermore, a 'confessional' poet courts death and destruction in order to arrive at a higher level of perception. Personal failure as well as mental illness is his favourite theme. The protagonist in a poetic piece feels quite alienated from the surroundings. Lastly, this brand of poetry is more often than not anti-structural, anti-elegant, and anti-establishment.

In his book, *The New Poets* (1967), M.L. Rosenthal, who gave a suitable title to the school of 'confessional poets' rightly points out that the best 'confessional' poetry is that which rises above the subject-matter to achieve a kind of victory over pain and defeat, poems which are glosses on the triumph of life. And Robert Phillips adds to this that "the best confessional poems are more than conceptions. They are revelations."[2] They are 'revelations' about their creator's personal vexations and predicaments.

Keeping in mind the above specifications about 'confessional' poetry and poets, it would be not wrong to characterize Kamala Das as a 'confessional' poet in the true sense of the term. Although she shows no signs of insanity or madness in her verse, as many 'new' American poets do, she exhibits all the essential features of a true 'confessional' poet. Henceforth in this chapter, we will try to discover these features in Mrs. Das's poetry and demonstrate how far she has gone in harnessing them.

There is too much of anguish and suffering in the verse of Kamala Das. It colours her poetic body through and through. The adverse circumstances have rendered her vision tragic and melancholy, — her upbringing by careless parents, her marriage with an egoistic and vainglorious man, her disappointment in love, and her illicit love-affairs with other men in order to remove her boredom and anxiety. Added to this, she is a very sensitive and unconventional woman, who is not prepared to be dictated terms. Her dissatisfaction in marriage and life sharpened her consciousness, and she possibly decided to air out her grievances through the poetic medium, because many unpalatable things can be said in this medium without incurring the wrath of powerful persons (who were rather shocked to read her revelations in *My Story*). Her autobiography in prose is more baffling and dazing than her poetry,

2. Ibid., p. 17.

though both speak about the same person and her woeful situation. In *Summer in Calcutta*, we have a poem entitled "Too Early the Autumn Sights," which clearly brings out her misery and sorrow:

Too early the autumn sights
Have come, too soon my lips
Have lost their hunger, too soon
The singing birds have
Left. (p. 26).

Another poem, "The End of Spring," also symbolically articulates the end of happiness and cheerfulness and the approach of the old age, disease and decay. In *The Descendants*, the poem "Substitute" is laden with the stings of 'blackmail and sorrow':

Life is quite simple now —
Love, blackmail and sorrow. (p. 6).

"The Conflagration" also highlights the poetess's silent suffering in the company of a cruel man. She asks herself:

Woman, is this happiness, this lying buried
Beneath a man? (p. 20).

In *The Old Playhouse and Other Poems*, the poem "Gino" offers us the following lines:

Perhaps some womb in that
Darker world shall convulse, when I finally enter,
A Legitimate entrant, marked by discontent.
(p. 14; *Italics mine*).

Examples of her 'discontent' and resultant convulsions and shocks may be multiplied easily, and the reader is left to judge for himself whether she is sad and anguished or not.

Kamala Das's poetry has a strong note of subjectivism, — the same sort of subjectivism as we witness in the Romantic poets of England (in Shelley and Keats particularly). The poetess is mostly concerned with herself as a victim of circumstances and sexual humiliations. In one place in *My Story*, she says, 'In the orbit of illicit sex, there seemed to be only crudeness and violence.' All her quest for true love lands in disasters of love. All her poetry is an expression of her private experiences in matters of love and sex. It operates from the level of the personal and the particular rather than from that of the general and the universal. There is a strong autobiographical touch in it. Thus, in *Summer in Calcutta*, we have the poem "The Dance of the Eunuchs" which corresponds to her own feeling of persecution and inadequacy. The eunuchs are depicted as under:

Some beat their drums; others beat their sorry breasts
And wailed, and writhed in vacant ecstasy. They
Were thin in limbs and dry; like half burnt logs from
Funeral pyres, a drought and a rottenness
Were in each of them. (p. 9).

The poem "The Freaks" highlights Mrs. Das's predicament as a married woman, who does the following on getting no true love:

It's only
To save my face, I flaunt, at
Times, a grand, flamboyant lust. (p. 10).

In *The Descendants*, we have the following poetic passage wherein her subjective feelings are predominant:

But,
I must pose,
I must pretend,
I must act the role
Of happy woman,
Happy wife.

("The Suicide," p. 2).

The lengthy poem, "Composition," also abounds in personal emotions and assumed roles. Herein Kamala says:

What I am able to give
is only what your wife is qualified
to give.
We are all alike,
We women,
in our wrappings of hairless skin. (p. 31).

In the third volume, the title-piece is a slight variation on the theme of illicit sex. The wife is treated no better than a hireling. She, therefore, loses her identity and personality, and suppresses her 'will and reason.' Her incurable malady finds a fine outlet in the following lines:

Cowering
Beneath your monstrous ego I ate the magic loaf and
Became a dwarf. I lost my will and reason, to all your
Questions I mumbled incoherent replies. (p. 1).

The poem "Glass" states clearly that finding no emotional identity or satisfaction with her man, Kamala is driven into others' arms:

I enter other's
Lives, and
Make of every trap of lust
A temporary home. (p. 21).

Consequently, her pure love degenerates into unwarranted 'lust,' and her emotional urges remain unfulfilled. Again and again, she focuses our attention on herself; again and again, she resorts to 'I' and 'my' and 'mine.' What can be a stronger proof of her 'subjectivism' than this?

Although a 'confessional' poet that Kamala Das is can make use of any subject for his treatment, he mostly confines himself to the regions of his own experience. By so doing he becomes very frank and honest, close and intimate, in his details. He hardly ever writes about 'old, unhappy, far-off things,' as Wordsworth and his band of followers did. That's why 'confessional' poetry sounds so appealing and so convincing. It frequently takes resort to personal failures and mental illnesses of its composer, and Kamala's verse is a brilliant illustration of it. In "My Grandmother's House," the following lines click:

I who have lost
My way and beg now at strangers' doors to
Receive love, at least in small change?

(*Summer in Calcutta*, p. 15).

The poet's failure in love is displayed in them. The poem "The Bats" brings out Mrs. Das's sense of sorrow and exhaustion in a striking manner:

From stranger to guest, from guest to
Lover, my beloved, when you take,
When you at least win, ignore the stain
Beneath dead eyes, the fatigue in my smile.

(*Summer in Calcutta*, p. 46).

"The Sunshine Cat" is a poem of her mental illness in the company of a cruel husband. In it we have:

Her husband shut her
In, every morning; locked her in a room of books
With a streak of sunshine lying near the door...
... ... ... ... ...
... ... ... ... when
He returned to take her out, she was a cold and
Half-dead woman, now of no use at all to men.

(*Summer in Calcutta*, p. 49).

Her hollow marital relationship comes under fire in the poem "Captive":

My love is an empty gift, a gilded
empty container, good for show, nothing
else.

(*The Descendants*, p. 17).

"Composition" brings to the fore the rottenness of her body and the uselessness of her love-pranks. In it she states:

> To be frank,
> I have failed.
> I feel my age and my uselessness.
>
> (*The Descendants*, p. 34).

"The Old Playhouse" offer us the following, reminding us of the sickening state of her mind:

> There is
> No more singing, no more a dance, my mind is an old
> Playhouse with all its lights put out.
>
> (*The Old Playhouse and Other Poems*, p. 1).

When the light of love is put out, an encircling gloom pervades the mind. This happens usually with a sharp, sensitive person like Kamala Das.

A 'confessional' poet often writes about death, disease and destruction. He is much concerned with the decay of the body and its aftermath effects. Mrs. Das's story has also been a story of recurrent attacks of diseases and illnesses. In her autobiography, we have several accounts of them. Chapter 32 of *My Story* offers us this: "After my return from home, I slipped into a phase of poor health and like a hibiscus shedding its dark petals my poor body shed red clots on the bathroom floor, and no amount of rest did it any good."[3] A gentle lady doctor took her to nursing home and there she recovered. Another account of her illness occurs in chapter 40 of her autobiography, which is given below:

> I had lost during that illness the resemblance to anything human. I looked like a moulting bird. My skin had turned dark and scaly. My voice had thinned to a whisper.... My little son was frightened of my looks and burst out crying. My second son tried for several days to rub mustard oil on my scaly legs to make me normal again.[4]

Chapters 47 and 48 contain description of another illness which completely broke her. She observes about this as follows: "I was physically destroyed beyond resurrection. But while my body lay inert on my sick bed, my mind leapt up like a waking greyhound and became alert."[5]

Kamala Das has written quite a few poems on decay, disease and death. Thus "The Fear of the Year" in *Summer in Calcutta* denotes,

---

3. *My Story*, p. 142.
4. *Ibid.*, p. 179.
5. *Ibid.*, p. 220.

symbolically, the approach of old age, after which she will be 'dead, dead, dead'. "Winter" and "The End of Spring" in the same volume are of similar nature. In "A Relationship" she mentions that she will have no escape from her pitiless husband and that she will find her rest, her sleep, her peace, and even her death only in his arms. The poem "Too Early the Autumn Sights" signifies early decay and subsequent cheerlessness of the poetess:

> Too early the autumn sights
> Have come, too soon my lips
> Have lost their hunger, too soon
> The singing birds have
> Left. (p. 26).

"The Sunshine Cat" metaphorically recalls the plight of Mrs. Das who feels 'half-dead' while living with her man. In "I Shall Some Day," she hopes to see her world someday when she will be de-fleshed, 'de-veined, de-blooded' and reduced to 'a skeletal thing'. For her, life has been death, and so real death will neither scare her, nor effect a change in her. This is what we find in "Death Brings No Loss." The second volume, *The Descendants,* has, on the whole, a more sombre atmosphere than the first one. In the opening piece, "The Suicide", the poetess expresses her desire to die when she is unable to find true love. She says:

> O sea, I am fed up
> I want to be simple
> I want to be loved
> And
> If love is not to be had,
> I want to be dead.... (p. 2).

The next poem, "A Request", carries her supplication to her people not to throw away her body on her death, but preserve it to have an evaluation of its 'worth' in life (p. 5). "Palam" is another poem dominated by the thought of decay and death:

> Walk away from me into lonely night
> With my finger-prints on you, my darling, go, while like
> blood
> Running out
> And death beginning, this day of ours is helplessly ending.
> (p. 10).

The poem "Contacts" also refers to 'that longer sleep,' and so is "The Maggots" with its 'corpse'. The closing piece of the volume, "Composition" mentions that the tragedy of life is 'not death but growth, and this 'growth5 is equivalent to 'death-in-life.' The third volume, *The Old Playhouse and Other Poems*, has a poem titled "After the Illness" which describes the poetess's serious illness and her survival:

> There was then no death, no end, but a re-uniting
> The weary body settling into accustomed grooves
> And, he said, his soft suffering face against my knee
> I know you would survive, my darling, I willed it so.
>
> (p. 50).

This poem, however, is remarkable in that it rises above mere considerations of physical decay and disease and attains a higher level of co-existence for her, since she is now loved for her spirit only, and not for her body.

As in the 'confessional' poetry in general, Kamala's verse distils emotions through the medium of free verse. Kamala knows the limitations of rhymed verses, and opts for *vers libre* to be able to articulate her 'open heart' for the benefit of her readers. Take, for example, the following:

> Love
> I no longer need,
> with tenderness I am most content,
> I have learnt that friendship
> cannot endure,
> That blood-ties do not satisfy.
>
> (*The Old Playhouses...*, p. 5).

Free verse as employed here offers immense opportunity for freedom of speech; it is also allied with elasticity and tenderness in expression. It does not require us to search for 'the best words in a best order' (Coleridge). Simplicity and spontaneity are its hallmarks. Kamala Das has also tried her hand at prose poems, though she has not written as many of them as Pritish Nandy. Two of the significant prose poems are: "The Swamp" and "Sunset, Blue Bird," which are placed at the end of the third volume. The following extract is taken from "The Swamp":

> my lover ageing without grace says why do you want my child i am your child yes yes yes then again and again this tragic sport that has made of us its addicts he undressing my soul effortlessly blindly reaching the locus of anguish but still i shake my head i leave unsatisfied for what does he bare for me on the bed in his study except his well tanned body.
>
> (*The Old Playhouse...*, p. 52).

The above extract may be marked as running without use of commas and full stops and capital letters, and gives a taste of the technique of American poet, E.E. Cummings.

Now, we come to the point that 'confessional' poetry is often anti-structural, anti-elegant, and anti-establishment, and that Kamala Das is also so in her poetry. While the extract cited above from "The Swamp" may be taken as an example of the anti-structural, we offer yet another example here to substantiate the statement. This is from "An Introduction":

In him...the hungry haste
Of rivers, in me....the oceans' tireless
Waiting. ... Anywhere and,
Everywhere, I see the one who calls himself
If in this world, he is tightly packed like the
Sword in its sheath.

(*The Old Playhouse...*, p. 27).

And this is not only an illustration of the anti-elegant, but also of the poetess's outspokenness and candour:

I run up the forty
Noisy steps to knock at another's door.
Through peep-holes, the neighbours watch,
They watch me come
And go like rain. ... ...
... ... ... ...
..., ask me why his hand sways like a hooded snake
Before it clasps my pubis. Ask me wrhy like
A great tree, felled, he slumps against my breasts,
And sleeps.

("The Stone Age," *The Old Playhouse...*, p. 51).

Both her approach to love and her account of it are anti-elegant and anti-stylish. And then, here is an illustration of the anti-establishment in Mrs. Das's verse:

I shall some day leave, leave the cocoon
You built around me with morning tea,
Love-words flung from doorways and of course
Your tired lust. I shall some day take
Wings, fly around, as often petals,
Do when free in air....

("I Shall Some Day," *The Old Playhouse...*, p. 48).

The 'cocoon' stands for 'establishment' of all sorts — for the bonds of marriage, family, and society, from which she wishes to 'fly' away.

In the end, Kamala Das is a typical 'confessional' poet who pours her very heart into her poetry. She is largely subjective and autobiographical, anguished and tortured, letting us peep into her sufferings and tortured psyche. Thanks to her that a reliable poetic voice has been heard in contemporary Indo-English verse at long last.

# 6

# Diction and Versification

## Diction

Kamala Das, who received no formal education, no pompous university degree, is a conscientious artist who is mainly guided by her impulse and instinct for precise and Harmonious words. She is fully aware of the value of words and their finer shades of meaning. She can make subtle distinctions in picking up or turning down her words and phrases. Like W.B. Yeats, she knows that 'words alone are certain good,' and like Nissim Ezekiel she believes that 'the best poets wait for words.' The choice words, phrases and expressions render her poetry beautiful and precise. Poets, held Yeats, are like women who 'must labour to be beautiful,' and here is a woman poet who has known through the years how to 'labour' and how to 'be beautiful.'

But being a poet of love essentially, Kamala Das sometimes feels that 'words' are a nuisance in love-making. In her poem, "Words," she acknowledges their natural growth on her like leaves, but she also says:

> But I tell myself, words
> Are a nuisance, beware of them, they
> Can be so many things....
>
> (*Summer in Calcutta*, p. 11).

Although she does not know the precise source of these 'words' — and in this quite unlike T.S. Eliot — she speculates that they possibly spring from 'a silence, somewhere deep within.' This speculation is like Tennyson's trying to locate the actual cause and the region of 'tears' in his poem "Tears, Idle Tears." As contrasted to this is the assertion of Eliot in his *Four Quartets*:

Words move, music moves
Only in time; but that which is only living
Can only die. Words, after speech, reach
Into the silence. Only by the form, the pattern,
Can words or music reach
The stillness, as a Chinese jar still
Moves perpetually in its stillness.

("Burnt Norton," *Collected Poems*: 1909-1962, p. 194).

What is missing in Mrs. Das is the philosophical certitude of T.S. Eliot. In another poem, "Convicts," Kamala once more pinpoints the futility of 'words' during and after intense love-making:

There were no more
Words left, all words lay imprisoned
In the ageing arms of night.

(*The Descendants*, p. 26).

Here the language of love becomes the language of darkness.

In her well-known poem, "An Introduction," Kamala speaks out her mind with regard to the question of the use of 'language.' Herein she writes about herself:

I am Indian, very brown, born in
Malabar, I speak three languages, write in
Two, dream in one. Don't write in English, they said,
English is not your mother-tongue. Why not leave
Me alone, critics, friends, visiting cousins,
Every one of you? Why not let me speak in
Any language I like? The language I speak
Becomes mine, mine alone. It is half
English, half Indian, funny perhaps, but it is honest,
It is as human as I am human, don't
You see?

and further:

It voices my joys, my longings, my
Hopes, and it is useful to me as cawing
Is to crows or roaring to the lions, it
Is human speech, the speech of the mind that is
Here and not there, a mind that sees and hears and
Is aware. Not the deaf, blind speech
Of trees in storm or of monsoon clouds or of rain or the

Incoherent mutterings of the blazing
Funeral pyre.

(*Summer in Calcutta*, p. 59).

This is a powerful plea for her use of the English language. Whether she 'dreams' in it or in Malayalam is shrouded in mystery, as Rahman also suggests, she 'writes' in English with an easy command and awful skill. "An Introduction" is more concerned with her use of 'English' and others' protest over it than with that of any other language. She has written a number of collections of short stories in her mother tongue undoubtedly, but her claim to English is no less. In a pert reply to the questionnaire of P. Lal in *The Miscellany* about the validity of English as a medium of poetic communication, she rightly states: "Why in English is a silly question. It is like asking us why we do not write in Swahili or Serbocroate. English being the most familiar, we use it. That is all."[1]

The diction of Kamala Das is, broadly speaking, lyrical and natural. Simplicity and lucidity are its hallmarks. It is hardly ever wrapped up in philosophical broodings or mystical abstractions. Mark her lyricism in the following passage:

It is I who laugh, it is I who make love
And then, feel shame, it is I who lie dying
With a rattle in my throat. I am sinner,
I am saint. I am the beloved and the Betrayed.

("An Introduction," *Summer in Calcutta*, p. 60).

The last three lines become incantatory and speak in the voice of an enraptured sage of the Upanishads. Here language has been put to an excellent use, and it does not fail the emotions of the poetess. The poem, "The Suicide," is a marvellous piece of lyricism and simplicity:

O sea, I am fed up
I want to be simple
I want to be loved
And
If love is not to be had,
I want to be dead,...

(*The Descendants*, p. 2).

With Sappho-like ecstasy and clarity of expression, she candidly lays bare her woman's heart when she says:

What I am able to give
Is only what your wife is qualified

1. *The Miscellany*, No. 32 (April 1969), p. XXXVIII.

To give.
We are all alike,
We women,
In our wrappings of hairless skin.

("Composition," *The Descendants*, p. 31).

The snare of womankind as a whole is exposed here in a tone of utter sincerity and fidelity.

Kamala Das's diction is marked also by a notable sweep and speed in its movement onward. The poem, "The Child in the Factory," presents a fine example of it:

Angry glow, that factory
Dies.
Half drunk with sleep,
And sick with lies, I obey,
I recognise,
I love.

(*Summer in Calcutta*, p. 30).

Sometimes the poetess uses the same word in different clauses of a sentence to achieve this objective. Thus, in "The Inheritance," she writes:

Oh God,
Blessed be your fair name, blessed be the religion
Purified in the unbelievers' blood, blessed be
Our sacred city, blessed be its incarnadined glory....

(*The Old Playhouse...*, p. 20).

The device, of repetitiveness has been adopted by her to suit the purpose and the velocity of emotion. Not only a certain words and phrases have been repeated, but a whole set of expression, nay a whole clause, is frequently resorted to. For this, one may look up "The Stone Age":

Ask me, everybody, ask me
What he sees in me, ask me why he is called a lion,
A libertine, ask me the flavour of his
Mouth, ask me why his hand sways like a hooded snake
Before it clasps my pubis. Ask me why like
A great tree, felled, he slumps against my breasts,
And sleeps. Ask me why life is short and love is
Shorter still, ask me what is bliss and what its price....

(*The Old Playhouse...*, p. 51).

In this poetic passage, 'ask me' has been repeatedly used. Some other poems prone to this device are: "Drama," "Substitute," "Radha," and "Composition." This is from "Substitute":

It will be all right when I learn
To paint my mouth like a clown's.
It will be all right if I put up my hair,
Stand near my husband to make a proud pair.
It will be all right if I join clubs
And flirt a little over telephone.
It will be all right, it will be all right
I am the type that endures.
It will be all right, It will be all right
It will be all right between the world and me.
It will be all right if I don't remember
The last of the days together....

(*The Descendants*, p. 6).

'It will be all right' has been used here again and again, even in the contents where the intentions of the poetess are juxtaposed. But what could be a better poetic tool than this for one who is highly sensitive and extremely emotional and one who has been leading a life of tension and restlessness?

The repetitive application of words, phrases and expressions makes Kamala's poetry truly musical and rhythmical. It was Hopkins, one of the greatest innovators in English prosody, who had stated that 'Rhyme removed, much ethereal music leaps in the air.' Kamala Das, who does not practise 'rhyme' in her verse, is a living example of 'much ethereal music'. Keeping apart such poems as "A Hot Noon in Malabar," "Radha," and "*Summer in Calcutta*," where we witness a cadence boom of repetition of words and phrases, her poetical pieces like "The Testing of the Sirens," "The Doubt," "Blood," and "Glass," offer us a feast of musical delight and harmony. Of these, "The Testing of the Sirens" contains the following moving lines:

Ah, why does love come to me like pain
Again and again and again?

(*Summer in Calcutta*, p. 64)

and "Glass" has the following:

A woman-voice
And a
Woman-small. I do not bother
To tell: I've misplaced a father
Somewhere, and I look
For him now everywhere.

(*The Old Playhouse...*, pp. 21-22).

The latter excerpt is specially to be marked for its internal rhythm — 'woman' in the middle of the first line becomes 'Woman' in the beginning of the third line. While the consonance of 'brother' and 'father' is so evident, the terms 'somewhere' and 'everywhere' have an arresting jingling sound born of internal rhythm. Kamala Das is an adept in moulding her words and expressions in a highly musical form. She does not delight in lilting cadence alone, but also in producing harsh and grating sounds. Take the following as an instance:

You dribbled spittle into my mouth, you poured
Yourself into every nook and cranny, you embalmed
My poor lust with your bitter-sweet juices. You called me
wife,
I was taught to break saccharine into your tea and
To offer at the right moment the vitamins. Cowering
Beneath your monstrous ego I ate the magic loaf and
Became a dwarf.

(*The Old Playhouse*....., p.1)

The frequent use of 'b', 'd' and 't' sounds and so many harsh and difficult words is to be found herein.

Kamala Das's poetry accommodates figures of speech in a befitting manner. Her alliteration breathes fire and fury at places. Mark the following passage for its alliterative quality:

Love-lorn,
It is only
Wise at times, to let sleep
Make holes in memory .....
..... ..... ....
.... .... the soul's mute
Arena,
That silent sleep inside your sleep.

("Luminol," *The Old Playhouse*..., p. 12).

There is no dearth of such passages in Das's verse, and they may easily be located in "An Introduction," "In Love," "Love," "Substitute," "The Suicide," "Composition," and "The Stone Age."

The use of simile by Kamala is excellent. "Drama" likens 'a red, red lamp' to 'an angry sun,' while "The Stone Age" compares the sway of 'his hand' to 'a hooded snake.' Another poem, "Forest Fire," has a remarkable application of simile:

Of late I have begun to feel a hunger
To take in with greed, like a forest-fire that
Consumes....

(*The Old Playhouse...*, p. 39).

The ferocity of her 'hunger' is compared to that of 'a forest fire.' The poems "Annette," "Convicts," "Gino," "Nani," etc. have also beautiful similes in them.

Kamala also makes use of metaphor in her verse in a noticeable manner. The short poetic piece, "Annette," offers us the following lines:

Annette,
At the dresser.
Pale fingers over mirror-fields
Reaping
That wheat brown hair.

(*The Descendants*, p. 12).

'Mirror-fields' and 'wheat brown hair' are touching metaphors in them. More touching is the following extract from "Substitute":

After that love became a swivel-door,
When one went out, another came in.

(*The Descendants*, p. 7).

'Love' is made 'a swivel-door' here, emphasising the frequent change of lovers indicated by the opening and closing of the door. It is definitely a powerful metaphor to give vent to the poetess's bitter sense of love-making and her disgust with it.

Occasionally, Kamala's diction tends to be aphoristic and maximatic, as in "Substitute":

Life is quite simple now —
Love, blackmail and sorrow.

(*The Descendants*, p. 6).

It immediately recalls T.S. Eliot to our minds who in his poem, "Fragment of an Agon," says:

Birth, and copulation and death.
That's all, that's all, that's all, that's all,
Birth, and copulation, and death.[2]

In case of Eliot, human life has been compressed into 'Birth, and copulation and death;' it is nothing more than this. Kamala's "Composition" is also aphoristic, especially in: 'The tragedy of life/ is not death but growth' (*The Descendants*, p. 29).

2. T.S. Eliot, *Collected Poems*, p. 131.

The diction of Kamala Das is rarely suggestive, since it is mostly 'expressive' in character. An 'expressive' language spares nothing for the fancy of the reader and speaks aloud all sentiments and thoughts in a hurried pace. But in a poem like "The Maggots" there is a tone of suggestiveness:

> At sunset, on the river bank, Krishna
> Loved her for the last time and left....
> That night in her husband's arms, Radha felt
> So dead that he asked, What is wrong,
> Do you mind my kisses, love? and she said,
> No, not at all, but thought, What is
> It to the corpse if the maggots nip?

(*The Descendants*, p. 22).

This short piece effectively suggests that Radha — no one else than the poetess herself — has lost her true, ideal love for ever, that her husband's offer of physical love to her is nothing but the 'nipping of the maggots' on her lifeless body ('corpse'). The language of suggestiveness begins to work in Kamala's poetry when she resorts to the Radha-Krishna myth to play it up as a vigorous symbol of genuine love.

The abundant use of imagery renders Kamala's verse pictorial and sensuous. It produces auditory, tactile and sensory effects on the reader, and sometimes he wonders whether he is not in the midst of Keats's poetry. Mark the concreteness and sensuousness of the following:

> ...How well I can see him
> After a murder, conscientiously
> Tidy up the scene, wash
> The bloodstains under
> Faucet, bury the knife...
> And, what am I in sex who shuttles
> Obsessively from his
> Stabs to recovery
> In her small silent room?

("The Doubt," *The Descendants*, p. 16).

The entire scene painted here is that of a copulation and afterwards. It contains descriptions of male and female participation in sex-act proper, and is full of eroticism and sensuality. Another poem which is more erotic and more sensuous almost like Keats's "The Eve of St. Agnes" and Coleridge's "Christabel," is Mrs. Das's "The Looking Glass." It partly runs as under:

Getting a man to love you is easy
Only be honest about your wants as
Woman. Stand nude before the glass with him
So that he sees himself the stronger one
And believes it so, and you so much more
Softer, younger, lovelier...Admit your
Admiration.

and further goes on:

Notice the perfection
Of his limbs, his eyes reddening under
Shower, the shy walk across the bathroom floor,
Dropping towels, and the jerky way he
Urinates. All the fond details that make
Him male and your only man. Gift him all,
Gift him what makes you woman, the scent of
Long hair, the musk of sweat between the breasts,
The warm shock of menstrual blood, and all your
Endless female hungers. (*The Descendants*, p. 25).

The 'fond details' furnished by the poetess, who herself has had long and exasperating experience of love and sex with her man, keep the reader spellbound unto the very last. She speaks of the 'nudity' of man and woman who are standing before a mirror and of their feverish and 'reddening' love-pranks.

**Versification**

Kamala Das, whose diction is essentially modern and surcharged with emotion, adopts a matching poetic technique to suit her purposes and the demands of our age. For the vigorous and sweepy expression of her verse, she did not need the artificial and gaudy technique of the school of Pope nor did she require the languid air and the love-lorn language of the Romantics; she rather needed the immense liberty and flexibility of the Modems like Ezra Pound, T.S. Eliot, the Sitwells, E.E. Cummings, Theodore Roethke, Robert Lowell, Sylvia Plath, and Anne Sexton. She, therefore, took resort to *vers libre* or free verse, which allowed her ample freedom of utterance in verse form, without letting the emotions slip off or their intensity slide off. In poem after poem, she applies the same technique, the same poetic tool. "The Sea Shore," "The Suicide," "Substitute," "Composition," "The Dance of the Eunuchs," "Blood," "The Stone Age" — in fact, majority of her poems — all employ *vers libre* in their texture, and here is being presented only one instance out of innumerable ones:

It was hot, before the eunuchs came
To dance, wide skirts going round and round, cymbals
Richly clashing, and anklets jingling, jingling,
Jingling...

("The Dance of the Eunuchs," *Summer in Calcutta*, p. 9).

What is to be noticed here is the fact that within a space of, say, three-four lines the poetess has spoken of no fewer things or persons — the season being 'hot' summer, the 'eunuchs' coming to dance, their skirts following their motions, their cymbals producing sweet sound, and their anklets jingling in their dance. This kind of description of varied details in such a small place is actually a gift of our scientific age, — a gift which is hardly witnessed in the previous eras. For example, we don't find this in Wordsworth's "The Daffodils," which calls up the following lines to describe the same flower:

Continuous as the stars that shine
And twinkle on the milky way,
They stretched in never-ending line
Along the margin of a bay;
Ten thousand saw I at a glance,
Tossing their heads in sprightly dance.[3]

What is being suggested here is that Mrs. Das's poem has greater scope for inclusion of details, whereas Wordsworth wastes his six precious lines on describing the mere physical appearance of the daffodils.

Blank verse is not Kamala's portion, but she tries her hand at prose poems occasionally. In The Old Playhouse and Other Poems, she has given us two poems written in the experimental style of E.E. Cummings. These two poems are: "The Swamp" and "Sunset, Blue Bird." In the former, we have:

in malabar during the rains after one singularly
dark week and one hot morning our backyard was
a swamp my feet cracked the grey crust and i sank
with a wail (p. 52).

and in the latter, we get:

...he no longer calls for me he no longer comes to
me or stands at the open window to smile at me but
everywhere i look i see him everywhere i do not
look i see him i see him in all i see him in everything
like a blue bird at sunset he flits across my sky.... (p. 54).

---

3. Cited from *Pages of English Poetry*, ed. P.E. Dustoor, 1979, p. 21.

These may be compared with any of the poems of Cummings, say, with the following:

'next to of course god america
i love you land of the pilgrims' and so forth oh
say can you see by the dawn's early my
country 'tis of centuries come and go....[4]

or, with the following:

since feeling is first
who pays any attention
to the syntax of things
will never wholly kiss you.... (*Ibid*,, p. 112).

But it may be added that Kamala Das's such poems are very limited in number, and hence she can't rank with Tagore or even with Pritish Nandy in this matter.

Besides the frequently used running lines to be had in Mrs. Das's verse, we come across a few exceptions in the forms of couplets and quatrains. "The Flag" in *Summer in Calcutta* is totally cast in couplets:

The orange stands for fire, for fire that eats
Us all in the end...
The white stands for purity that we dream of and
Never find (p. 21).

But the neat arrangement of ideas in two lines here does not compare favourably with the perfect heroic couplets of Dryden or Pope. As Kamala is not highly educated, she may not possibly know the subtle nuances of a couplet, and it is to her credit that she does not follow the great masters in this regard. Similarly, her arrangement of lines in four for a stanza, as seen in "Someone Else's Sons" (*Summer in Calcutta*, p. 31)), does not subscribe to the traditional practice (as in P.B. Shelley's "To A Skylark"). This also applies to her poem "Three P.M." (*The Descendants*, p. 21).

Evidently, Kamala Das is not as great an innovator in English as G.M. Hopkins or E.E. Cummings was, but she has emotions arrested in glowing words and phrases and expressions and she has skill to turn out brilliant images and similes, and these are enough to qualify her as a genuine poet in English. She is more interested in the 'spontaneous overflow of powerful feelings' than in introducing new things in the art of versification. The distinguished English poet, Geoffrey Hill, was right to remark that "the one poet who stood out in P. Lal's *Modern Indian Poetry in English: An Anthology and a Credo* (1969) was Kamala Das" as Devinder Kohli informs us.[5]

4. Cited from *American Poetry of the Twentieth Century*, ed. Richard Gray (Cambridge: Cambridge Univ. Press, 1976), p. 112.

5. D. Kohli, *Kamala Das* (1975), p. 26.

One critic who has severely lashed at Kamala Das, the poet, is Linda Hess. Writing in 1966, Hess remarked as follows:

> There are major weaknesses in Mrs. Das's book.
>
> These can be characterized as a general carelessness in composition, a looseness typified by the alarming number of ellipses, three lazy dots thrown in at the end or middle of a line and seeming to say, 'This matter could be elaborated much further, but I lack either the wit or the energy to do it.' There are frequent repetitions of words and phrases, another quick solution to the problem of filling up a line but one that has disastrous effects on intensity and precision. There are patches of triteness and lapses of balances. Too often the end of a line brings an unnatural break in the diction which seems to have no excuse except the whim of the author.

But Hess was also quick to perceive 'the original poetic voice' in Mrs. Das, saying —

But all these deficiencies cannot finally cloud the fact that a genuine poetic talent is at work here. It lives on every page, is woven even through the most distressingly flawed poems. And in a few superb pieces it stands forth unchallenged and unmistakable.[6]

Even a liberal critic like Devinder Kohli, however, finds something missing in Kamala Das, especially with the second volume of verse. Kohli notices "a falling-off in The Descendants (1967)"[7] Miss Vimala Rao feels that Kamala's first volume is 'the best' to date. To me, these scholars rub on the wrong shoe, and it would have been more reasonable on their part had they pointed out her successively deserting Muse and her gradual shifting to prose.

In the end, Prof. K.R.S. Iyengar rightly recognises Kamala Das as "one of the most aggressively individualistic of the new poets" whose fiercely feminine sensibility enables her "to articulate the hurts it has received in an insensitive largely man-made world."[8] Prof. Iyengar maintains that Mrs. Das gives "the impression of writing in haste," but that she reveals "a mastery of phrase and a control over rhythm — the words often pointed and envenomed too, and the rhythm so nervously, almost feverishly, alive."[9] If Das's rhythm is 'feverish' her diction is charged with powder and her versification is technically accomplished.

---

6. *Quest* (April-June 196b), p. 38; cited by Devinder Kohli.
7. Kohli, *op. cit.*, p. 25.
8. K.R.S. Iyengar, *Indian Writing in English*, 1973, pp. 677-80.
9. *Ibid.*, p. 680.

# 7

# Imagery and Symbolism

The noted English poet, Housman, once remarked of 'imagery' as follows: 'Here is poetical gold; take it! Here is radiant beauty; be moved.' Imagery tends to serve twin-purposes together — that of 'ornamentation' and that of arousing 'aesthetic pleasure' in the reader. An image enables a poet to convey his abstract thoughts or mystical longings in a 'concrete' form. It evokes a picture, a 'concrete' idea or shape, about the writer's feelings. F.R. Leavis, a reputed English critic, has observed that "*tone* and *attitude towards* are likely to be essential heads in analysing the effects of interesting metaphor or imagery, and that "Whenever in poetry we come on places of especially striking 'concreteness'—places where the verse has such life and body that we hardly seem to be reading arrangements of words — we may expect analysis to yield notable instances of the co-presence in complex effects of the disparate, the conflicting or the contrasting."[1] The process of 'image-making' involves the skilful use of metaphors, similes, contrasts, and may be equated to 'picture-making' or 'concretization of emotions.'

As a poet, Kamala Das makes ample use of images and symbols. Some of these images are so recurrent that they become symbols in her poetry, but it must be added here that they are not too many. A study of her imagery and symbolism is bound to reveal her artistic skill and craftsmanship, and hence it is both relevant and rewarding. Henceforth we will examine some of her dominant and recurrent images and symbols.

Kamala Das makes a hectic search for true love in her poetry, and her personal predicament gets reflected in it. She is a poetess of love and sex and of the body. One of the dominant images in Mrs. Das's poetry is that of 'the human body.' She celebrates it like the American poet, Walt

1. Leavis, "Imagery and Movement," *Twentieth Century Poetry* (1975), p. 33.

Whitman, and regards it as a gift of God to the human race. It is often viewed in two aspects — male and female. While the male body is a source of corruption and exploitation, the female body is a storehouse of beauty and chastity misused to the maximum. Here is a subtle analysis of the male physiology made with an aversion:

He talks, turning a sun-stained
Cheek to me, his mouth, a dark
Cavern where stalactites of
Uneven teeth gleam, his right
Hand on my knee ... ...
... ... ... ...
... ... Can't this man with
Nimble finger-tips unleash
Nothing more alive than the
Skin's lazy hungers?

("The Freaks," *Summer in Calcutta*, p. 10).

Evidently, the poetess has drawn an ugly picture of the love-lorn man, who has 'a sun-stained cheek,' 'a dark cavern' in mouth, and 'uneven teeth' protruding forward. She is not happy in his company and complains thus:

You dribbled spittle into my mouth, you poured
Yourself into every nook and cranny, you embalmed
My poor lust with your bitter-sweet juices.

("The Old Playhouse," *The Old Playhouse and Other Poems*, p. 1).

These lines evoke the image of saturation in sex-act, but all the same they highlight her sense of bitterness in his contact. The poem "The Stone Age" is also an expression of her dislike of the man, and in utter despair she cries out:

Ask me everybody, ask me,
What he sees in me, ask me why he is called a lion,
A libertine, ask me the flavour of his
Mouth, ask me why his hand sways like a hooded snake
Before it clasps my pubis. Ask me why like
A great tree, felled, he slumps against my breasts,
And sleeps.

("The Stone Age," *The Old Playhouse...*, p. 51).

She does not relish 'the flavour of his mouth' and the way he clasps her 'pubis.' All this is conveyed by the image of 'a hooded snake,' which is a dangerous thing. Whether she likes him or not, he thrusts himself upon her in a mood of frenzied passion. This is contained in the image of 'a great tree, felled.' Naturally, he is very heavy for her, and yet he 'slumps' against her breasts and 'sleeps' in their warmth. Through the arresting images Kamala Das has made it amply clear that he is largely a man of lust and cruelty, having no regard for her own feelings. Again and again, she raises her voice against his physical love. In the poem "Convicts," she says thus:

> That was the only kind of love,
> This hacking at each other's parts
> Like convicts hacking, breaking clods
> At noon. We were earth under hot
> Sun.

(*The Descendants*, p. 26).

This richly suggestive poetic passage tells us immediately about his lustful nature and the violent sexual involvement of both in the summer season. On the part of the poetess, there is a sense of guilt over such an involvement conveyed by the metaphor 'convicts.' The proper sexual act involving energy and speed is marvellously carried through by the image in 'breaking clods/At noon.' The phrase 'breaking clods' suggests that there was a kind of grating sound while they were copulating. The word 'earth' indicates their 'earthiness' as well as their 'reception of the heat of the burning sun.' And there could be no better image to express the energy and the violence in the sexual intercourse than that of 'hot sun.' ft is creditable to Kamala Das that she makes the natural elements serve her ends, and here at least she succeds admirably in it.

The above illustrations should not lead one to believe that Kamala always hates the body. On the contrary, she sometimes conveys her pleasures experienced in the company of her lover. She is not only a beloved seeking restlessly the sources of 'true love,' but also a wife legally wedded to and socially bedded by a man and a mother of three loving children. In the poem "Winter," she frankly admits:

> And, I loved his body without shame,
> On winter evenings as cold winds
> Chuckled against the white window panes.

(*Summer in Calcutta*, p. 17).

Winter being a cold season, she turns to her man without masks or pretensions to derive warmth and vitality in his living contact. *My Story*, her autobiography, also reveals the fact that she surrendered herself to her husband after long illness in a spirit of total abandonment. A poem like "The Music Party" gives vent to her desire of looking at her man unashamedly before things go wrong for her:

I wish my
Eyes were similarly
Brave and had looked at you
At least once before the
Singing stopped and you left
Quickly, without goodbye....

(*Summer in Calcutta*, p. 34).

The poem "The Looking Glass" underlines her ecstasy of union with her man. It is a woman in love who is saying the following lines:

Notice the perfection
Of his limbs, his eyes reddening under
Shower, the shy walk across the bathroom floor,
Dropping towels, and the jerky way he
Urinates. All the fond details that make
Him male and your only man.

(*The Descendants*, p. 25).

Another poem, "A Relationship," brings to the fore her dire necessity of the man. She writes:

Yes,
It was my desire that made him male
And beautiful, so that when at last we
Met, to believe that once I knew not his
Form, his quiet touch, or the blind kindness
Of his lips was hard indeed.

(*Summer in Calcutta*, p. 18).

Here the acceptability of the man is quite obvious. She is also aware of the charms of her body, the power of her physical appeal, and speaks of it unequivocably in some of her poems. In "Loud Posters," we have:

I've stretched my two dimensional
Nudity on sheets of weeklies, monthlies,
Quarterlies...

(*Summer in Calcutta*, p. 23).

"The Looking Glass" is matchless in this context; it is a poem of utter honesty and plain-speaking on the part of the poetess. Mark how she portrays the softer charms of a woman in it:

> Getting a man to love you is easy
> Only be honest about your wants as
> Woman. Stand nude before the glass with him
> So that he sees himself the stranger one
> And believes it so, and you so much more
> Softer, younger, lovelier...Admit your
> Admiration.

and further:

> Gift him all,
> Gift him what makes you woman, the scent of
> Long hair, the musk of sweat between the breasts,
> The warm shock of menstrual blood, and all your
> Endless female hungers.

(*The Descendants*, p. 25).

The poetess conveys here the power that a woman holds, and her idiom is fundamentally modernistic instead of being romantic or idealistic as in the previous ages. For her, a partner is essential in sex-drama, just as she is essential for him in a life of real enjoyment.

Keeping the above facts in mind, it may be said that Anisur Rahman is only partly correct when he observes that Kamala Das "views the male body as an agent of corruption," and that she also "regards it as a symbol of corrosion, the destroyer of feminine chastity."[2] He is rather nearer the truth when he later remarks that "She is aware of both the beauties and crudities of the male body,"[3] since here he is not adopting a partisan attitude. A truth is that which emerges triumphant in the ultimate analysis, and Rahman's first statement crumbles in the light of this test. The image of the human body is employed so frequently that confusion creeps up in a few minds, but there is no confusion whatsoever with regard to its being a symbol for the poetess. And as a symbol, it is both a destroyer and a preserver, both a source of death and a source of life, for her.

Another recurrent image in the poetry of Kamala Das is that of 'the sun.' This image has, though, been used frequently, it has not been imparted "a systematic symbolism." It has been employed as "an agent of scorching heat, corruption and lust."[4] It is often associated with the heat generated by sex and the drabness of life. It affects the skin and makes it tanned and stained, as we find it in "The Freaks" — 'He talks, turning a

2. A. Rahman, Expressive Form in the Poetry of Kamala Das, p. 38.
3. Ibid., p. 42.
4. Ibid., p. 44.

sun-stained/Cheek to me.' The poem "In love" equates the 'burning' sun with the 'burning' mouth of the man in love:

Of what does the burning mouth
Of sun, burning in today's
Sky remind me...oh, yes, his
Mouth.....

(*Summer in Calcutta*, p. 14).

In "Sepia," the sun is presented as a source of 'scorching' heat that dries up the very marrow of the bones. It is conceived as a destroyer of the real charms of life:

It's time to hold anger
Like a living sun
And scorch,
Scorch to the very marrow
This sad-mouthed human
Race.

(*Summer in Calcutta*, p. 24).

The image of the sun as evoked here is not benevolent; it does not illumine the world of the poetess, but rather consumes it. The oppressive power of the sun is to be felt in "The Dance of the Eunuchs" and "Summer in Calcutta;" its 'wildness' is to be witnessed in "A Hot Noon in Malabar." It contributes richly to the atmosphere of the poems — the pitiable condition of the dry-ribbed eunuchs, the misery and depression of the poetess herself, and her eventual relief through love and sex. The image of the sun in the poem "Summer in Calcutta" is highly charged with sensuousness and sensuality. This is what we find in it:

What is this drink but
the April sun, squeezed
Like an orange in
My glass? I sip the
Fire, I drink and drink
Again, I am drunk,
Yes, but on the gold
Of suns

and further:

Dear, forgive
This moment's lull in
Wanting you, the blur
In memory.

(*Summer in Calcutta*, p. 48).

Explicitly, the 'drinking' and the state of being 'drunk' of the poetess bears an added significance in the light of what she says in the second quoted excerpt. In the poem "The Sunshine Cat," the sun becomes a companion of the forlorn and the helpless, but it offers her no health or comfort in her depressing situation; she is rather left 'a cold and/Half-dead woman.' Some other poems wherein this image is employed are: "The Pigeons," "Drama," "Punishment in the Kindergarten," "The Conflagration," and "Convicts." The poem "The Conflagration" makes use of this pervasive image as a symbol of either passion or unwilling sexual indulgence. The poems "The Testing of the Sirens" and "In Love" are also rich in sexual overtones, but in "The Conflagration" the image denotes the poet's own willing participation in sex:

> We came together like two suns meeting, and each
> Raging to burn the other out. He said you are
> A forest-conflagration and I, poor forest,
> Must burn.

(*The Decendants*, p. 20).

Her participation in sex removes her loneliness and langour temporarily. She possibly knows that sex is the source of all life, the vital principle of all existence, but also that her partner is nothing more than an expert in arousing 'the lazy hungers' of the body. This does not provide her with long-felt and much-needed emotional gratification. Both the 'burning sun' and the male body signify for Kamala Das the same thing — the oppressive force of lust and the resultant decay and destruction.

Partly related to the sun is the image of 'darkness' in the poetry of Mrs. Das. Obviously, this image is not so pervasive as the sun, and hence it does not attain the status of a symbol. Usually it is linked with 'sleep,' which also implies 'longer sleep,' *i.e.*, death. We have it brilliantly used in the poem "Death Brings No Loss":

> Each night when darkness turns
> Me blind, I think of death,
> Understanding it to
> Be like night-fall, just a
> Temporary phase, which
> Brings no loss.....

(*Summer in Calcutta*, p. 61).

Darkness is an attribute of the night, and the night is the right time of physical contact between the opposite sexes. This has been conveyed in the poem "The Testing of the Sirens":

The night, dark-cloaked like a procuress, brought
Him to me, willing, light as a shadow,
Speaking words of love
In some tender language I do not know....

(*Summer in Calcutta*, p. 63).

The metaphor 'procuress' generates a bad taste in the passage, and the poetess does not like his arrival in the night for the satisfaction of the flesh. Occasionally, darkness signifies the 'womb' of the mother. In "Afterwards," we have:

Son of my womb,
Ugly in loneliness,
You walk the world's bleary eye Like a grit.

(*Summer in Calcutta*, p. 55).

Kamala Das is no philosopher to be concerned with the pre-natal existence of her son, and so like an ordinary mother she imagines that he must have sprung from the dark. Her motherly experience is again expressed in "Jaisurya" in softer terms:

Only that matters which forms as
Toadstool under lightning and rain, the soft
Stir in womb, the foetus growing....

(*The Descendants*, p. 27).

Here 'lightning and rain' stand for the ferocity and saturation in sexual intercourse, which is not so meaningful for her as the conception of a child through it. Mrs. Das's wifely stance may be questionable, but her motherly stance is *not*.

One of the most predominant images in Kamala's poetry is 'the sea,' the recurrent use of which accords it the status of a symbol. The image serves the purpose of a retreat from the scorching world of the sun. Devinder Kohli rightly suggests that the sea-imagery is "part of Kamala Das's elemental symbolism," and that it is "related both to her moods of anguish and release."[5] The longer poem, "Composition," depicts her childhood memory of the sea as 'the wind's ceaseless whisper in a shell' which changes into the sound of 'the surf breaking on the shore.' The sea was within a walking distance — only two miles away — from her Malabar house. It provides her with rest and comfort and a life of 'uninvolvement':

All I want now
is to take a long walk

5. Kohli, *Kamala Das*, p. 32.

into the sea
and lie there, resting,
completely uninvolved.

Her attraction for it, she clarifies onwards, is 'a childish whim,' a thing associated with her dreamy past:

But,
rest is only a childish whim,
a minor hunger.
Greater hungers lurk
at the basement of the sea.

(*The Descendants*, p. 34).

'Greater hungers' point to the elemental hungers of love and sex. Another longish piece wherein this image turning into a symbol operates so forcefully is "The Suicide." In this piece the sea is made an associate of 'the soul' discarding 'the body' away:

I throw the bodies out,
I cannot stand their smell.
Only the souls may enter
The vortex of the sea.
Only the souls know how to sing
At the vortex of the sea.

(*The Descendants*, p. 1).

The 'sea' is the bedroom for her 'swimming.' As a child, she had swum into it; as an adult, she again wishes to swim into it and thereby quench her thirst for emotional contentment. She says:

O sea, I am happy swimming
Happy, happy, happy....

(*The Descendants*, p. 2).

She knows that 'water' is the prime mover of life, signifying the procreating power of the mother. That's why it is easy for her to 'hold' it, but it is pretty difficult to 'hold' the love of her man. Her desire for fidelity in love and sex has been shattered by him and this makes all the difference in her life. She cries out in pain and dejection:

Holding you is easy
Clutching at moving water,
I tell you, sea,
This is easy.
But to hold him for half a day

Was a difficult task.
It required drinks
To hold him down.

(*The Descendants*, p. 3).

In a way, she herself is the holder of 'water,' as she, too, is a mother yearning for peace, happiness and security. But her 'water' is not sufficient for a drunkard like him, and so he needs 'drinks' to make himself warm and jubilant. Towards the close of the poem, her identification with the sea is so obvious:

O sea,
You generous cow,
You and I are big flops
We are too sentimental
For our own Good.

(*The Descendants*, p. 4).

Both are 'generous' and 'sentimental,' which accounts for their being 'big flops.' This identification was totally lacking in the image of the sun.

The sea-imagery also occurs in so many other poems of Kamala Das, in such poems as "The Invitation," "Convicts," "The Joss-Sticks at Cadell Road," and "The High Tide." But in these poems it is only 'a secondary image' and does not become a symbol at all. In "The Invitation," the sea is depicted as 'garrulous':

The sea is garrulous today. Come in,
Come in ... ... ...
Oh Sea, let me. Shrink or grow, slosh up,
Slide down, go your way,
I will go mine.

(*The Descendants,* p. 14).

Besides, the 'tides beat against the walls,/they beat in childish rage.' The garrulity of the sea and the beating of the tides against the walls signify the waves of emotion welling up in the poetess's heart, for she asserts that she is not afraid of 'dying' (a metaphor often used for the consummation of love). The poem "The High Tide" is also of identical nature. Here the sea is analogous to the rising passion within her:

It's only the wind knocking at the door, the sea
Is wild this morning, there is perhaps a high tide on....

(*The Old Playhouse...*, p. 43).

In expressing her emotion through the imagery of the sea, the poetess is quite natural and simple. The natural phenomenon she used to observe from her childhood comes handy to serve her poetic purpose in a remarkable fashion. In the poem "The Joss-Sticks at Cadell Road," the sea becomes a receptacle of 'the poor men's bodies,' which burn like joss-sticks. On the whole, the poem stresses the futility of the physical love. In the poem "Convicts," the poetess evokes the image of the post-sexual experience in the dark room through the sea.

Kamala Das also makes use of the four natural elements in her poetic art. These four elements forming an integral part of her imagery are: the fire, the earth, the water, and the air. Of the four, the 'fire' image is the most powerful and appealing. In *Summer in Calcutta*, the poem "The Flag" employs it brilliantly:

> The orange stands for fire, for fire that eats
> Us all in the end.... (p. 21).

The fire-image immediately strikes us as a destroyer of the human body. The noted English poet, T.S. Eliot, also employed it in his poetry as a symbol of both the physical love of the self and the celestial love of the Divine. His "Little Gidding" has been characterized as 'a poem of fire.' Kamala Das used this image as a destroyer of the human body as well as of human passion. Her poem "The Sea Shore" shows it in its role of a destroyer, and so is her "Forest Fire." In the latter poem, we have:

> Of late I have begun to feel a hunger
> To take in with greed, like a forest-fire that
> Consumes.... (p. 51).

The image of 'fire' and 'heat' is conspicuous in two of her most important poems — "The Dance of the Eunuchs" and "A Hot Noon in Malabar." It tends to create a proper atmosphere for the poetic utterance. The latter poem offers us the following lines:

> Yes, this is
> A noon for wild men, wild thoughts, wild love. To
> Be here, far away, is torture. Wild feet
> Stirring up the dust, this hot noon, at my
> Home in Malabar, and I so far away.... (p. 47).

The overpowering 'heat' has stirred her emotions so 'wildly' that they are almost uncontrollable. The repetitive use of the word 'wild' actually denotes the ferocity and impetuosity of her passion at noon.

The air-image is to be found in "The Conflagration." Here Mrs. Das writes:

> Fetter that ominous wail.
> Let only silence move there humming a slow
> And Languid air.
>
> (*The Descendants*, p. 20).

But the poem is more inclined towards the fire-image. The last stanza bears it out:

We came together like two suns meeting, and each
Raging to burn the other out. He said you are
A forest-conflagration and I, poor forest,
Must burn. But lay on me, light and white as embers
Over inert fires. Burn on, elemental
Fire, warm the coal streams of his eternal flesh till
At last, they boiling flow, so turbulent with life.

It gives title to the poem and sets its tone and temper. An atmosphere of 'burning' and 'boiling' is created here due to the meeting of two lovers.

There are some other poems in which all the four elements figure simultaneously. Such poems are "Afterwards," "An Introduction," and "Convicts." In "Afterwards," Kamala Das writes:

The earth we nearly killed is yours
Now. The flowers bloom again,
But a savage red; it takes
Time to forget blood or the quick gasps
Of the dying. And the sudden pain,
But the sun came again, and rain.

(*Summer in Calcutta*, p. 56).

The 'earth' here stands for the calm, quiet existence of the poetess before she entered into a sexual intercourse with her man. The blooming flowers and the dying attain an additional meaning and significance when they are considered in this light. The 'blood' and 'the quick gasps' are attendant upon the proper sexual act. The 'sudden pain' is the throes of delivery, while 'the sun' and the 'rain' are, in this context, welcome signs of son-birth and sprinkling of the holy water around. The poem "An Introduction" also employs all the four elements in its texture. In it the poetess says:

Not the deaf, blind speech
Of trees in storm or of monsoon clouds or of rain or the
Incoherent mutterings of the blazing
Funeral pyre.

(*Summer in Calcutta*, p. 60).

Another beautiful application of the four elements is to be had in "Convicts." In it the poetess writes:

Darkness we grew as in silence
We sang, each note rising out of

Sea, out of wind, out of earth and
Out of each sad night like an ache....

(*The Descendants*, p. 26).

Here the poetess suggests that her 'ache' and sadness is something like an inalienable part of the universe.

There is also the image of the 'bird' in the poetry of Kamala Das. Though this image is rarely employed by her, it does find a place in her verse. It does not, however, attain a symbolic significance. In the poem "The Stone Age," we have the following:

You turn me into a bird of stone, a granite
Dove, you build round me a shabby drawing room....

(*The Old Playhouse...*, p. 51).

This image is mostly used for bondage and oppression. 'The poetess desires freedom from her 'fond husband,' whom she calls an 'old fat spider,' and the world of wifely responsibilities created by him, but she helplessly feels that she is like a bird in the cage. The self-same idea finds an outlet also in the poem "I Shall Some Day," wherein Kamala says:

I shall someday take
Wings, fly around, as often petals,
Do when free in air ....

(*The Old Playhouse...*, p. 48).

The imagery here derives its efficacy and sustenance from the world of birds. The terms 'wings' and 'fly around' leave us in no doubt.

Kamala Das has turned Indian myths, occasionally, into symbolistic imagery, and one such myth is the Radha-Krishna syndrome. The myth assumes the shape of a recurrent symbol in her poetry. When she looks around, and discovers a vast gap between the real world and the world of her dreams, she becomes pessimistic in her outlook upon life and applies this myth as a symbol for her salvation. In My Story, she writes:

> There was an imaginary life running parallel to our real life. I filled his (her son's) childhood with magic and wonder. Always he smiled with the sheer happiness of being alive. He sat on my knee looking like the infant Krishna.[6]

and again:

> Free from that lust of human bondage, I turned to Krishna. I felt that the show had ended and the auditorium was empty. Then he came, not wearing a crown, not wearing

6. *My Story*, p. 114.

> make-up, but making a quiet entry. What is the role you are going to play, I asked Him. Your face seems familiar. I am not playing any role, I am myself, He said. In the old playhouse of my mind, in its echoing hollowness, His voice was sweet. He had come to claim me, ultimately. Thereafter he dwelt in my dreams. Often I sat crosslegged before a lamp reciting mantras in His praise.[7]

These passages confirm her unflinching devotion to Lord Krishna, whom she often remembered and praised in hours of her duress. Such passages are numerous in her autobiography. All the poetical volumes of hers contain references to Krishna and Radha. Unrequited in love, she becomes Radha seeking the divine love incarnate as Krishna. In the poem "Radha-Krishna" in *Summer in Calcutta*, the poetess displays her aversion for physical love, which is the only type of love that her man knows. In another poem, "Radha," she identifies herself with the Lord, and says:

> And virgin crying
> Everything in me
> Is melting, even the hardness at the core
> O Krishna, I am melting, melting, melting
> Nothing remains You ....

(*The Descendants*, p. 9).

There is a highly moving poem, "Ghanashyam," in the collection *Tonight, This Savage Rite* (1979), which highlights the poetess's deep love for Krishna. In it she writes;

> Ghanashyam,
> You have like a koel built your
> Nest in the arbour of my heart.
> My life, until now a sleeping jungle
> Is at last astir with music.

Her devotion to Lord Krishna has eventually made her happy and contented. Thus, mythical symbol has come to her rescue at long last and saved her from a life of utter dejection and suffering.

---

7. Ibid., p. 195.

# 8

# Tragic Vision

A thorough investigation of Kamala Das's poetry reveals that her vision is essentially tragic and pessimistic. Instead of a robust optimism of the kind of Robert Browning, we find a tragic outlook behind her work of the kind of G.M. Hopkins (minus his religious fervour) and Thomas Hardy. Right from the beginning of her life, things and events began to shape adversely for her. As a child, she was not properly cared for along with other children; as an adult, she fell into the company of an unsympathetic and insensitive husband (see her *My Story* for a reaffirmation). The inevitable result was that the black shadows of a crippling world around her began to darken her dreams of a happy, settled life. Her childhood innocence got shattered by the terrifying experiences of the adult world. She couldn't receive love, in its true sense, at the legitimate sources, and her sense of attachment was never fulfilled. All these factors combined to turn her gloomy and melancholy in her outlook upon life.

'The hero of a tragedy,' observes Freud in *Totem and Taboo*, 'had to suffer; this is today still the essential content of a tragedy.' Suffering and unhappy ending are still considered as its essential ingredients, according to Indian as well as Western theoreticians of aesthetics. If these ingredients are discovered in poetry, as in case of the poet under discussion, tragedy does not remain a monopoly of the theatre. Explicitly, poetry can also order itself into a tragic or comic pattern. Kamala Das's poetry abounds in details of misery and grief, loneliness and helplessness, death and disease, coldness and frigidity, frustration and dejection, and all these[1] render her vision tragic.

Even Das's prose works, especially *My Story*, affirm her being an artist of tragic vision. Manasi, the protagonist of Kamala's novel, *Alphabet*

1. We will substantiate this statement later on by offering illustrations from her poetry.

*of Lust*, later repents for her blunders in abandoning her happy and contented domestic life and in aspiring for political powers. She feels for her deserted husband, Amol Mitra, and her neglected daughter, Supama. Mark how the novelist subtly portrays her mental tortures and self-loathing:

> We are mere puppets in the hands of God, said Amol and although the sentence would have at once irritated Manasi at one time, she now felt that Amol was right. Perhaps there was a God. A power higher than even the Prime Minister. She hated herself then. How despicable I have become, she whispered into Amol's ears as he kissed her throat. He shook his head vehemently. No, Mano, you are as lovable as you always were, he said.[2]

The happiness lost at home can hardly ever be regained in the outer world. This is the realisation of Manasi, who has reached the highest rung of her political career, and this is also the feeling of Kamala Das, the novelist. There are strong autobiographical reflections in this novel which immediately remind the reader of Sylvia Plath's *The Bell Jar*.

*My Story* offers several passages confirming the view that Kamala Das is a writer of tragic outlook with little hopes of redemption. After her engagement with her finance, Kamala went to Calcutta to live with her parents, and when some time passed, the young man was invited to Calcutta for a week's stay, but he could not offer any happiness or consolation to her. This situation is described in Chapter 21 of the autobiography:

> My cousin asked me why I was cold and frigid. I did not know what sexual desire meant, not having experienced it even once....It was a disappointing week for him and for me....I wanted conversation, companionship and warmth. Sex was far from my thoughts. I had hoped that he would remove with one sweep of his benign arms the loneliness of my life....
>
> I did not know whom to turn for consolation.[3]

For her coldness and frigidity, one should also look up pp. 91, 92, 93, 94-95, 103, 107-108, 109, etc. Speaking of her ruinous loneliness, Kamala writes:

> As I wrote more and more, in the circles I was compelled to move in, I became lonelier and lonelier.

2. *Alphabet of Lust*, pp. 143-144.
3. *My Story*, p. 87.

> I felt that my loneliness was like a red brand on my face. In company when there were dinners at any friend's house, I sat still as a statue, feeling the cruel vibrations all around me. Then my husband realised my plight and stopped taking me out anywhere.[4]

That she had to make compromises in life and exist in a state of utter helplessness and hopelessness is expressed beautifully in the following passage:

> I did not have the educational qualifications which would have got me a job either. I could not opt for a life of prostitution, for I knew that I was frigid...I was a misfit everywhere. I brooded long, stifling my sobs....[5]

The sentence 'I was a misfit everywhere' paints a very gloomy 'picture about her. Nothing could offer her comfort and solace, and her miseries went on multiplying day by day. Once she suffered a serious nervous breakdown, as her husband would not allow her freedom of movement and action. Added to this was her delicate health which invited diseases frequently and allowed death to haunt her mind. When she returned to Malabar after honeymooning with her husband in Bombay, her condition was pitiable:

> My grandmother wept when she saw me. She called an Ayurvedic physician to get me examined for illness which may have seized me in Bombay. Under his treatment and in the care of my grandmother, I forgot my miserable honeymoon days and became healthy once more.[6]

During another illness, she became very weak and lost all energy in her — "I was physically destroyed beyond resurrection."[7] These illnesses had rendered her so gloomy and dispirited that death began to dangle before her like a living reality. In the last chapter (50th), she says:

> I have been for years obsessed with the idea of death. I have come to believe that life is a mere dream and that death is the only reality. It is endless, stretching before and beyond our human existence. To slide into it will be to pick up a new significance. Life has been, despite all emotional involvements, as ineffectual as writing on moving water. We have been mere participants in someone else's dream.[8]

---

4. *Ibid.*, p. 186.
5. *Ibid.*, p. 109.
6. *Ibid.*, p. 95.
7. *Ibid.*, p. 220.
8. *Ibid.*, p. 230.

The obsession with 'the idea of death' made her a spent force, almost a dead wood, even in the midst of resourceful persons and modern amenities of life.

Like her prose, Kamala's poetry also unfolds the tmth of her plight and tragedy. All her poetical volumes contain flashes of her miserable lot and hopeless condition. In *Summer in Calcutta*, she says in one of her poems thus:

Who can  
Help us who have lived so long  
And have failed in love?

("The Freaks," p. 10).

Here is recorded "the woman's impatience and frustration with the man as well as the moment: with the man because of his sexual passivity and slackness and with the moment because it mocks her feminine integrity," observes D. Kohli.[9] The poem "The Fear of the Year" highlights Mrs. Das's obsession with decay and death. In "My Grandmother's House," she explains with sorrow:

I who have lost  
My way and beg now at strangers' doors to  
Receive love, at least in small change? (p. 15).

Betrayal in marriage and love forms the theme of "A Relationship." The poem "The End of Spring" signifies the end of the charming season of love and the birth of the wintry season of 'fear' and hatred:

What is the use  
Of love, all this love, if all it gives is  
Fear, you the fear of storms asleep in you  
And me the fear of hurting you? (p. 20).

Frustration is at the root of the poem "Loud Posters," and Kamala identifies herself here with the 'typewriter,' a machine having no individuality since all typewriters 'click' alike. She articulates her resentment over the 'sad' lot of humanity in "Sepia."

Let anger grow like a living sun  
And scorch,  
Scorch to the very marrow,  
This sad-mouthed human  
Race. (p. 25).

9. Kohli, *Kamala Das*, p. 64.

Like "The End of Spring," the poem "Too Early the Autumn Sights" signals the approach of decay and old age, which has killed her appetite and her singing spirit. Herein she writes:

Too early the autumn sights
Have come, too soon my lips
Have lost their hunger, too soon
The singing birds have
Left. (p. 26).

She strongly protests that the people recognise her by a particular name, — the name borrowed from another person, from her husband. The protest is a clear-cut indication of the failure of her marriage, telling heavily on her nerves and crushing her badly under its weight:

You ask of
Me a silly thing. Carry
This gift of a name like a corpse and
Totter beneath its weight
And perhaps even fall...I who love
This gift of life more than all! (p. 28).

So much crushed is she that she does not recognize her own voice, her own song, in the poem "Someone Else's Song." Her heart is broken, and she starts wailing at her personal predicament:

My heart — the wretched thing — is today
Cold, like those pale green mirrors
One sees in corridors....
("With Its Quiet Tongue," p. 32).

Her loneliness is marvellously brought out in "The Corridors":

Why do I so often in
Dreams linger at strange doorways,
Lonely to the bone, feeling
Like on impostor.... (p. 36).

Almost at every step she feels 'the loss of love' she actually never received (p. 40). Her deep-rooted anguish surfaces in the poem "The Bats":

My soul today is on its blinded, most
Frightened flight, like a bat that finds itself
In an alien zone of light. (p. 46).

Her husband's maltreatment comes out vividly in "The Sunshine Cat":

Winter came and one day while locking her in, he
Noticed that the cat of sunshine was only a

Line, a hair-thin line, and in the evening when
He returned to take her out, she was a cold and
Half-dead woman, now of no use at all to men. (p. 49).

The 'cat' is actually a symbol of the poetess herself who was an object of mistrust and humiliation at the hands of her own man. What could be a greater tragedy in personal human relationships than this? Kamala Das wanted 'freedom' in speech, action and movement, but that was denied to her by the earthly husband. Her desire for 'freedom' finds an outlet in the poem "I Shall Some Day." Another poem, "Death Brings No Loss" speaks a lot about her miserable life:

Each night when darkness turns
Me blind, I think of death,
Understanding it to
Be like night-fall, just a
Temporary phase, which
Brings no loss, for what was
Here before sun-down will
Be here tomorrow when
Light shall reveal it. (p. 61).

Living in such a horrible state, life and death become indistinguishable for her. When life is no more than a dark circle of routine and restriction, it is no better than death. The last poem of the volume, "The Testing of the Sirens" forcefully expresses her utter loneliness and disappointment. In one place in this poem, she says:

With the crows came the morning, and my limbs
Warm from love, were once again so lonely... (p. 63)

and in another:

Ah, why does Love come to me like pain
Again and again and again. (p. 64).

The repetitiveness in the second quoted extract reinforces the idea that there is no escape for her from the painful existence she is in, and that her 'pain' mainly springs from the unrequited love.

The same tone and temper may also be witnessed in *The Descendants* and *The Old Playhouse and Other Poems*. In them we have a number of poems highlighting the poetess's misery and grief, frustration and failure, frigidity and coldness. Thus, in The Descendants, we have a well-known poem called "The Suicide," which offers us the following:

O sea, I am fed up
I want to be simple

I want to be loved
And
If love is not to be had,
I want to be dead... (p. 2).

One of the most moving poems is "A Request", which is simple and straightforward in expression. It denotes that life has been worthless for Kamala Das, that love has totally deserted her. In great anguish, she says:

When I die
Do not throw the meat and bones away
But pile them up
And
Let them tell
By their smell
What life was worth
On this earth
What love was worth
In the end. (p. 5).

The poem "Substitute" also brings out her deep sense of sorrow and frustration:

Life is quite simple now —
Love, blackmail and sorrow. (p. 6).

She feels sorry and frustrated because "We have spent our youth in gentle sinning/Exchanging some insubstantial love" ("The Descendants," p. 8), and because "this day of ours is helplessly ending" ("Palam," p. 10). In "The Invitation," she writes:

I have a man's fist in my head today
Clenching, unclenching...
I have got all the Sunday evening pains. (p. 14).

Love is a great tragedy for her. The love that she receives from her husband is nothing but "an empty gift," "a gilded/empty container, good for show" ("Captive", p. 17). She, therefore, asks her woman-persona as under:

Woman, is this happiness, this lying buried
Beneath a man?

("The Conflagration," p. 20).

She wants to be liberated from the bonds of her man. The poem "The Joss-Sticks at Cadell Road" conveys this feeling of hers. At long last, she is left with no option but decay and die bitten by inner pulls and pressures. The poem "Composition," a longish piece indeed, expresses her bitterness over her failure and uselessness:

To be frank,
I have failed.
I feel my age and my
Uselessness. (p. 34)

and further:

my only freedom being
the freedom to
discompose. (p. 35).

In the latter passage, the word 'discompose' connotes 'get destroyed,' 'be dissolved.'

The third volume of Kamala Das has only fourteen new poems, others being taken over from the previous two volumes. Of these 'new' poems, "The Old Playhouse" conveys the poetess's deep sense of sorrow and remorse at surrendering herself to her man's physical demands and annihilating her own personality. She says:

Cowering
Beneath your monstrous ego I ate the magic loaf and
Became a dwarf. I lost my will and reason, to all your
Questions I mumbled incoherent replies.

The inevitable result is that she has landed into an inescapable tragedy:

There is
No more singing, no more a dance, my mind is an old
Playhouse with all its lights put out.
(*The Old Playhouse and Other Poems*, p. 1).

Time and again, Mrs. Das lodges her complaint against the same person, — the person who is responsible to have broken her completely in love. She is, therefore, fully aware of the 'withering' of her body, of the joylessness of her days:

This body that I wear without joy, this body
Burdened with lenience, slender toy, owned
By man of substance, shall perhaps wither battling with
My darling's impersonal lust. Or, it shall grow gross
And reach large proportions before its end. (p. 14).

She is distressed at the inhuman behaviour of her husband towards her. For him, she is nothing more than a toy of enjoyment, and she pays him in the same coin:

With a cheap toy's indifference
I enter other's

Lives, and
Make of every trap of lust
A temporary home. (p. 21).

She compares herself to a 'broken glass.' She wants to 'cry' when he mates her, but is helplessly tied to him:

Why
Did I
Not cry then, broken glass, beware? (p. 21).

The illness was the only time when she met him in a mood of surrender and abandonment — this is what we learn from My Story. The poem "After the Illness" also indirectly confirms it, since he is shown here as loving her for "perhaps the hidden soul" (p. 50). But barring her serious illness in the city of Bombay, she was almost always ill at ease with him. Immediately after, we have the poem "The Stone Age," which not only spurns his advances towards her but also spits out her venom at him:

Fond husband, ancient settler in the mind,
Old fat spider, weaving webs of bewilderment,
Be kind. You turn me into a bird of stone, a granite
Dove.... (p. 51).

In "The Swamp," she recollects him as "the richest the strongest the deadliest" man on earth (p. 53). And the last poem of the volume, "Sunset, Blue Bird" paints his betrayal and loss of love towards her (p. 54).

The foregoing survey of Kamala Das's verse reveals the fact that she is a deeply distressed woman, languishing for true love, repenting her hollow marriage, complaining of her man and situation. The circumstances she is placed in warrant a tragic vision of life for her. She has clarified as to what she implies by 'tragedy':

The tragedy of life
is not death but growth,
the child growing into adult
and, growing out of needs,...

("Composition," *The Decendants*, p. 29).

As for 'death,' she is never afraid of it, like John Donne; the last chapter of *My Story* makes it abundantly clear. 'Childhood' is ever associated for her with endearing memories, but 'adulthood' has totally battered her. Her hopes of a happy, married life and her dreams of a peaceful house flooded with love and laughter have been irrepairably shattered. She feels that she is of no 'use' as a grown-up woman, except as an object of pleasure for a possessive man and as a caretaker of his kids and kitchen. This is precisely what she states in the following in her autobiography: "Tragedy is not death but growth and the growing out of needs."[10] What kind of vision, if not tragic and pessimistic, is expected of a sensitive writer who holds such a conviction? It is, finally, all the more creditable to Mrs. Das that she has unfurled this vision in a beautiful 'poetic,' which is also 'expressive' (to use Rahman's word), form.

10. *My Story*, p. 119.

# 9

# Some Gems of Das's Poetry

In this chapter, we shall be dealing with some of Kamala Das's best-known poems. The selection of these poems being arbitrary may possibly be challenged, but they are undeniably the cream of her poetic produce. The poems to be critically studied here are the following:

(a) The Freaks,
(b) My Grandmother's House,
(c) A Hot Noon in Malabar,
(d) The Sunshine Cat,
(e) The Invitation,
(f) The Looking Glass,
(g) The Old Playhouse,
(h) An Introduction.

We shall now begin with the first one.

**(a) The Freaks**

This remarkable lyric is extracted from *Summer in Calcutta* (1965), and is to be marked for its abnormally psychological situation in love-making and its unredeemed helplessness and deep despair. The title itself suggests these things. The 'freak' is one who is capricious and whimsical in behaviour, one who does not behave in accordance with the accepted norm. The title suggests that the lovers — the woman and her man — do not behave properly with each other, and hence are abnormal and whimsical in their approach to love.

'He' in the poem is the man persona and 'Me' is the woman persona. They are together in a room. The lover talks and turns his reddened face towards her. But he is not like the lover in a fairy tale; he is rather repulsive to her. His cheeks are 'sun-stained' and brownish in colour; his mouth is ugly and looks like a 'dark cavern;' his teeth are 'uneven' and calciferous. Evidently, these details are given here to show the woman's disgust with the man. She seems to be tied to him socially, though personally she does not like him. Thomas Gray in his famous elegy written in a country churchyard was deeply moved by the loss of so many precious lives in villages whose talents were not properly utilized. Kamala Das in her poem expresses her ideas against arranged marriages which are usually inspired by the parents' conveniences more than those of the couples. The poetess, therefore, paints an abhorrent picture of her man, with whom she has to enter into sexual intercourse willy-nilly for his satisfaction. In such a situation, no partner feels happy and jovial. Except for physical contact, it offers no emotional contact between the man and the woman. Hence, her deep sense of personal agony and despair. Her situation becomes all the more pathetic because there is no escape from it. She is utterly helpless and hopeless.

The man puts his hand on her knee in an apparent gesture of love-making. And though they are inclined to make love to each other, they simply can't do so, because their minds, or at least the woman's, wander away. The phrase 'puddles of desire' denotes that the lovers are smitten by the arrows of love, but that their love is full of dirt and filth, and not pure and emotional. Where there is no meeting-point for the two hearts, the minds will definitely go astray. This is precisely Kamala's own situation, — a situation that Devinder Kohli characterizes as "a rather helpless situation."[1]

The woman-persona is filled with utter disgust at the failing of her lover, who can touch her with nimble finger-tips to fondle and soothe her, but who can offer her nothing more than 'skin's lazy hungers.' Possibly her sexual hunger also remains unfulfilled, nothing to speak of the yearnings of the heart for truer love and closer understanding. The fulness of life through "the sexual titillation and fulfilment"[2] has completely evaded her. So, in great despair, she asks the question:

> Who can
> Help us who have lived so long
> And have failed in love?

The heart remains 'an empty cistern,' and like a dry well devoid of the waters of life it harbours only 'coiling snakes of silence.' As a result, her impatience touches a new height. The man remains largely passive

1. Kohli, Kamala Das, p. 63.
2. M.L. Sharma, *Kamala Das*, p. 12 (A Punjabi University Publication — Correspondence Course Directorate).

and slack, mocking at her 'feminine integrity.' She has, therefore, to don the masculine role and flaunt 'a grand, flamboyant lust' at times in order to save her femininity. Though her lust is grand and flamboyant, it is not real and genuine.

There is, however, a sentence which is rather baffling — 'I am a freak.' This indicates that she alone is abnormal in the given circumstances, but the truth is she plays the male part of activity in sex-participation due to the laziness and passivity of her man. Her 'freakishness' is, therefore, boom of the passivity of her husband, who also is 'freakish' in not behaving like a natural man. The sentence also points to the woman's own deficiency in sexual indulgence as contrasted to the virility and storminess of the man's passion. Lest she should be taken as a sterile woman, who is incapable of love and sex, she occasionally flaunts 'a grand, flamboyant lust.' This role of 'flamboyant lust' is actually a 'freak' role, a masquerade, and it is possibly an extremist role put on by a woman of unfulfilled desire.

The poem contains some beautiful and yet difficult words and phrases, such as 'sun-stained/Cheek,' 'a dark cavern,' 'stalactites of/ Uneven teeth,' 'willed,' 'tripping,' 'puddles of desire,' 'nimble fingertips,' 'unleash,' 'Skin's lazy hungers,' 'An empty cistern,' 'coiling snakes of silence,' 'flaunt,' and 'a grand, flamboyant lust.' The images used in it suggest an overpowering sense of dejection and rejection on the part of the sexually conscious woman. The images are contained in 'sun-stained cheek,' 'puddles of desire,' 'an empty cistern,' and 'coiling snakes of silence.'

The diction is charged with fire and fury. The very opening strikes us with the phrase 'a sun-stained cheek.' The poem opens on a casual note. As usual, it is marked by 'dots' and 'dashes,' a characteristic fault of the style of Kamala Das as pointed out by Hinda Less. The tone is suggestive throughout, as one may easily recognise through several questions asked. The 'dark cavern' may signify the deep passion of the lover, who specializes in giving her the pleasures of skin and flesh and nothing more.

*stalactites* — a white growth on the roofs of caves as a result of calcium going up along with water vapour.

*unleash* — unchain, unfasten, let loose.

*Skin's lazy hungers* — physical passion; sexual titillation.

*An empty cistern* — An instance of visual imagery for an empty heart. 'Cistern' means 'water-tank.'

*flaunt* — show off.

*flamboyant* — gaudy, showy, blazy.

## (b) My Grandmother's House

This is one of the nostalgic poems first published in *Summer in Calcutta*. It is 'nostalgic' because it portrays the happy, carefree days of the poetess when she was a child (before her marriage). She yearns for the return of those days. In Malabar, she used to live in the aristocratic parental home which was affectionately supervised by her grandmother. The tone and the attitude of the poetess is the same here as those of Charles Lamb in his famous essay, "Old Familiar Faces." The poem also recalls Lord Tennyson's "Tears, Idle Tears" to our minds in 'thinking of the days that are no more.' The permanent departure of the dear and near ones marks all these literary pieces, whose dominant mood is one of melancholy and pathos and nostalgia.

Like the poem "A Hot Noon in Malabar," this one attempts to recapture and sustain the poetess's childhood memories. Kamala provides us detailed information regarding the genesis of this poem. In Chapter 33 of *My Story*, she writes:

> After the sudden death of my grand-uncle and then that of my dear grandmother the old Nalapat House was locked up and its servants disbanded. The windows were shut, gently as the eyes of the dead are shut.
>
> My parents took my great grandmother to the house called Sarvodaya where she occupied noiselessly the eastern bedroom on the ground floor, shaded by the tall mango trees through the leaves of which was visible the old beloved house. The rats ran across its darkened halls and the white ants raised on its outer walls strange totems of burial.[3]

The grandmother has been a source of affection and inspiration to the poetess, but her death has rendered her sorrow-stricken and desolate. The house looks totally deserted, now inhabited by snakes and rats. Kamala feels lonely and depressed. During one of her serious illnesses — during her nervous breakdown in the noisy city of Bombay — she had taken shelter in Malabar and was nursed back to perfect health by her anxious grandmother, but, alas, she is now no more alive. The expression 'blind eyes of windows' and 'the frozen air' reinforce the idea of death and desperation.

The grandmother's house is associated with an impenetrable sense of security and protection, which is now missing in her married life.

---

3. *My Story*, pp. 147–48.

Even the 'darkness' of this house kept security for her instead of terror or violence. Kamala rather wants that darkness to be lifted bodily and shifted to her new married home flooded with light (but with no security). She expresses this feeling of hers through an evocative image:

> pick an armful of
> Darkness to bring it here to lie
> Behind my bedroom door like a brooding
> Dog....

A 'dog' is a trusted companion keeping an unerring eye on the door to scare away the strangers and the enemies and to safeguard the inmates with all main and might.

The last few lines are addressed to the 'darling,' to her husband. Kamala tells him that:

> I lived in such a house and
> Was proud, and loved....

How nostalgic and pathetic these lines are! The sense of pride and love she once had in the house of her grandmother is now no more her property, since she has become a beggar for love who knocks helplessly at strangers' doors to receive it at least in a small measure. She has lost her way in quest of true love. This situation is in utter contrast to her previous life lived in the soothing company of her grandmother. Kamala tells us that she has often remembered her "Sweet frail great grandmother,"[4] and has remembered her with a sense of nostalgia and beggarliness. That her present life is sans love, sans pride, is emphatically conveyed by her begging for love at 'strangers' doors.' There can possibly be no worse pathetic situation for a married woman than this.

*withdrew into silence* — sank into silence.

*turned cold like the moon* — became very chilly, like the moon.

*blind eyes of windows* — coloured curtains or window panes. It also suggests an overpowering sense of death on the part of the poetess, and in this is not different from the 'frozen air' that follows.

*a brooding Dog* — is a visual image of a watchful and wary sentinel.

Mark the utter simplicity of the diction and the feeling in this poem as contrasted to those in "The Freaks."

4. *My Story*, p. 208 (ch. 45).

**(c) A Hot Noon in Malabar**

This poem, like "My Grandmother's House" is reminiscent of Kamala Das's childhood spent in her happy home in Malabar. It is picked up from *Summer in Calcutta* (1965). Tinged with pathos, the poem moves between memory and desire, between nostalgia and estrangement. It is certainly full of moving pathos and tenderness.

Apparently, the woman-poet is now living in a big city, far removed from her ancestral home. At noon, she is inside her house, but outside the world is none-too-happy. The beggars come and knock at the door raising unpleasant voices; the men from the hills pour in with parrots in cages and with dirty and stained clothes to tell fortunes of others; the dark-skinned Kurawa girls catch hold of the palms of their customers and please them with their sing-song voices; the bangle-sellers sell their bangles of varied colours. All of them have come from a long distance and have, therefore, developed cracks on their heels, so that when they ascended the porch of her city house, a grating noise arose.

The hot noon draws strangers to her porch who peep into her room through the window-drapes. Since they have sun-stained eyes, they can't see properly what is there inside. Getting disappointed there, they turn to the brick-ledged well to quench their thirst and feel some respite from the scorching sun. These strangers are usually doubtful at everything they look at; they are dark and silent and recalcitrant. When they speak, their voices sound unfamiliar and wild. In the unusual heat, wild men, wild thoughts, wild love consummate. Suddenly, the poetess is reminded of her parental home in Malabar, where things were quite different, though the people stirred about in the hot noons there as elsewhere.

There is only one sentence in the whole poem which marks a transition in the thought-sequence of Kamala; it is 'To/Be here, far away, is torture.' 'This sentence is pregnant with meaning and significance, for her 'torture' is linked up with the dusty and noisy city, whereas in her previous home of childhood she was all happy and content, with nothing to bother about. The 'hot noons' were essentially different in Malabar. In one piece, she rightly remarks: 'From every city I have lived, I have remembered the noon in Malabar with an ache growing inside me, a homesickness.'

The poem is, thus, a descriptive piece in the main, and reads exactly like a prose piece. In fact, as a prose piece it would have been much better, much more lucid and coherent. But as it stands, it is not free from syntactical and stylistic lapses, and it also abounds in dots and dashes.

There is too much emphasis on 'strangers' and one wonders what poetic purpose they serve where they stand. It may also be observed that the lines that click are the last ones. There is too much of artifice than art in it.

The poem is conspicuous for its autobiographical element. The details of locale, of persons and places, have been recorded literally in Kamala Das's autobiography. The 'cool black floor,' for instance, mentioned in it tallies exactly with the one mentioned in *My Story* (p. 17). Even the details of her various love-affairs can easily be corroborated from the records of her life. Similarly, her observations regarding her grandmother, her parental house in Malabar, the frigidity of Nalapat women in sexual matters in general, and the great stress and strain under which she somehow carried on her life: all are fine flashes of her autobiography.

For one thing, Kamala Das expresses her deep distrust and despair at the city-bred life, which cramps the elemental life-force. As contrasted to the city-snobs, those bom and bred in the open lap of Nature or even in the midst of jungles — such as the 'strangers' she speaks of in this poem — are much more favourably inclined towards this life-force. In *My Story*, she writes: "I should never have taken to wearing the coloured clothes of the city — I belonged to the serenity of Nalapat. Nalapat belonged to me. By abandoning it to the care of the vulgar caretakers and managers, I had hurt the spirit of the house. *I had unwittingly spilt the blood of its spirit....*"[5]

*whining* — long-drawn (voices).

*All stained with time* — All ravaged and rubbed by Time.

*Kurawa* — a caste of fowlers, basket-makers, and fortunetellers.

devouring rough/Miles — walking a long distance with difficulty and pain.

*Clambered up* — climbed up with difficulty.

*grating* — harsh, jarring.

*window-drapes* — window-curtains.

*peer in* — look inside, see inside, searchingly.

*brimming with the sun* — flooded with the sunlight, and hence blinded.

*the brick-ledged well* — the well having a ledge of bricks.

5. *My Story*, p. 209.

### (d) The Sunshine Cat

This poem, too, like the previous ones, finds a berth in *Summer in Calcutta* (1965). It is sans warmth, sans love. Sexual humiliation, which forms the main theme of Kamala Das's autobiography, *My Story*, is the central experience herein. It recounts the tale of a woman too much wronged by the male world around her.

The poem directly highlights the miseries of a forlorn woman. The men treated her very badly, — the man she loved did not reciprocate her feelings and he was basically 'selfish' and 'coward;' the husband, who neither 'loved' her nor 'used' her, but who was 'a ruthless watcher,' was also made of the same grain; the 'band of cynics' she ultimately turned to for her emotional gratification was all selfish and egotistic. These cynics with monkey-like hair on their chests subjected her to all kinds of humiliation and torture, including physical and odorous; their smells were sickening and they were mostly driven to her for quenching their raging lusts. All of them assured her to be 'kind' towards her, but they also pointed out to her that she was not meant for love, suggesting thereby that she was probably frigid and cold and ill-suited for love-making. When she got out of their clutches, she retired to her room, to her soft bed, and started sobbing and weeping. She now realised that 'tears' were her trusted companions and that she would have to pass the rest of her life in a sad, hopeless manner. At this moment, when she needed the love and consolation of her husband, he treated her with cruelty. He used to lock her up, every morning, in a room of books with a streak of sunlight lying near the door, before he went out for his official duty. Soon winter came and while locking her one day he realised that his woman was a mere skeleton, a hair-thin line, and no human creature of flesh and blood. By the time he returned to her in the evening, she was 'cold' and 'half-dead,' quite unfit for the touch of men. The disease hinted here 'is that of serious nervous breakdown, to recover from which Kamala Das had to go to her grandmother's.

The story of the genesis of the poem and other details related to it are to be found in Chapter 41 of *My Story*.

This chapter is titled "I withdrew into the cave I had made for myself." In it the writer first complains of the unsympathetic attitude of non-writers towards a writer, and then of her own aching loneliness. Speaking of the non-cooperative attitude of the non-writer, Kamala writes: "The essence of the writer eludes the non-writer. All that the writer reveals to such people are her oddities of dress and her emotional excesses." And a little onward, she writes again:

> As I wrote more and more, in the circles I was compelled to move in, I became lonelier and lonelier.
>
> I felt that my loneliness was like a red brand on my face. In company when there were dinners at any friend's house, I sat still as a statue, feeling the cruel vibrations all around me. Then my husband realised my plight and stopped taking me out anywhere.
>
> I withdrew into the cave I had made for myself where I wrote stories and poems and became safe and anonymous. There were books all round me, but no friend to give me well-meaning advice, no relative telling me of my discrediting my family-name, by my unconventional ways of thinking....[6]

The above passage quoted at some length amply shows the helpless and hapless situation of Kamala Das in her Bombay home. It stresses her utter loneliness and frustration, with no one to counsel or guide her.

This situation has been beautifully portrayed in the present poem. She has not received love from her licit or illicit orbits; she is totally lonely and frustrated. Those who claimed to be kind towards her had only subjected her to humiliation and injury. Her husband has been no better to her. He rather uses his matrimonial prerogative and shuts her in the reading room. She is, thus, completely isolated, and the only companion for her is the 'sunshine.' She is no better than 'the sunshine cat,' all pale and diseased. That is why the title of the poem is suitably chosen to be "The Sunshine Cat." The title is suggestive enough; it rather works as a symbol for her total isolation in the midst of material comforts. 'Cat' may also signify "the healthy and exuberant sexuality with which we normally associate this animal." Taken in this light, the poetess's life overbrimming with sexuality finds no true source for fulfilment, and it, therefore, becomes all the more miserable and deplorable. The last lines in particular and the tener and tempor of the whole poem in general verify this fact — 'now of no use at all to men.'

And then, the poem is pervaded with the air of lust and passion. It has no place for pure and true love. The poetess might feel a hunger for the ideal lover, but she cannot be freed of the sin of committing adultery with other men, and she seems to cry over the loss of her 'use' for men in general. The modern woman's predicament is energetically voiced in this poem, but her challenge of the socio-moral laws, nay her flauting of them, is unpardonable. In most of the poems of Kamala Das, the reader

---

6. *My Story*, p. 186.

is forced to believe that she has written them for sensational effects, but a healthy literature makes him wiser, healthier and happier. Put to this test, the poem fails to satisfy us, and the poet also falls fiat without any hope of redemption.

There are certain felicitous expressions in the poem, and the poet is at her best there. Because what we should expect of the poet is her capability of springing surprises through visual, arresting expressions rather than the profundity of thought in her. One such impressive expression is the men's 'chests where/New hair sprouted like great-winged moths.' It is decidedly born of her close observation of the male chests. Another remarkable expression is 'I shall build walls with tears,' and this 'wall' will effectively 'shut me in.' A third expression of impressive visual imagery is 'A yellow cat.' Was it not T.S. Eliot who had beautifully used the 'cat' image in the beginning of his immortal song, "The Love Song of J. Alfred Prufrock?" In its effectiveness and impressiveness the 'yellow cat' of Kamala Das comes very close to that of Eliot rubbing its nose against the foggy window-panes.

*a ruthless watcher* — a merciless observer (*i.e.*, the husband).

*the band of cynics* — the group of crazy people.

*sprouted* — shot forth, put forth.

*burrowing* — hiding, concealing.

*pegs of sanity* — drinks of rationality (*i.e.*, so far she was a sensible woman).

*a streak of sunshine* — a ray of the shining sun.

**(e) The Invitation**

This poem was included in *The Descendants* (1967). It is in the form of an interior monologue. It is a dialogue between the poetess and the sea, but the solo voice is that of the former. The 'tides' are nothing but the emotions welling up in the poetess. The dominant mood in it is one of death by drowning. The sea-image is so insistent here as in several other poems of the volume, *e.g.*, "The Suicide," "Substitute," "Ferns," "The Joss-Sticks at Cadell Road," etc. The poetic persona is in great despair due to failure in love and married life, and she receives an invitation from the sea to commit suicide in order to escape the trials and tribulations of existence. The invitation for death or suicide is so urgent and strong, but she resists it by throwing up courageous suggestions of her own, by reminiscing the happy moments of her past life lived with her husband, by holding out promises of better life in the future, and by overcoming the invitation for self-destruction eventually.

The poem opens with a very touching image of meaningless sexual encounters of the poetic persona (a woman indeed). The image shows a male fist 'clenching and unclenching' in her head. The intensity of her 'Sunday evening pains' in her head is remarkably suggested by it. On Sundays when her husband is at home, her headache becomes intense and throbs in the same way as the frequent closing and opening of an ugly male fist.

In the meantime, the sea extends its invitation to her by becoming 'garrulous' that she should come down and drown herself into it. Moreover, her life has been empty and deserted, and so her 'dying' won't make much difference. And if she dies, the sea will become richer to contain her.

But the woman-persona turns down the suicidal suggestions of the sea. She asks it to go its way, while she will go her own. She prays to the sea to leave her alone. Suddenly she remembers the lover who came to her for a brief rest and refreshment after a busy schedule, as a fish comes out of the water for a puff of breeze. He was warm in her arms for a while and did not talk much to produce a jarring sound. The sea, however, reminds her that she was thinking of the past, which is a sort of disease, and that the man has gone away for ever. It would be, therefore, foolish to wait for him; instead, she should accept its invitation and be free of all worldly botherations. But again, she refuses to oblige it, for she still remembers her lover and his warm embraces. While he was with her on the bed, which had become a shrunken paradise for them, they derived utmost pleasure. Walking out together, they made the whole city look a blessed paradise on earth. The sea is still insistent with her and invites her again. It urges her to have herself drowned into it. This will be a cool, carefree death for her — much different from the death by burning on a funeral pyre. As contrasted to this, the cool, sandy bed of the sea will provide her great relief like the soft pillows for a reclining head. But she again remembers her lover and his pleasant company. The two used to pass their summer afternoons on beds together and experience the sexual pleasures unspeakably. The heat of the summer had rendered their bodies inert and indolent, but the sexual contact expanded their private cells. Getting a little dejected, the sea once again cries out for her and asks her to stop thinking of bygone days. It tells her that it has waited for long for 'the right one' to come, 'the bright one' to live in its blue waters. The woman-persona says 'no' to the call of the sea, telling it that:

I am still young
And I need that was for construction and
Destruction. Leave me....

The sea may pry into and violate the sanctity of her private life, but it will not be allowed to gain by her losses. She is not prepared to die at all. The sea now grows angry and wild; it starts beating against the walls of her home in a childish rage. She can't withstand it, and so asks for the forgiveness of her lover to join the sea. After all, how long can one resist such a beating?

The poem highlights the staggering situation of a middle class wife in the clutches of male domination. It externalizes the poetess's hapless condition in a loveless family. That her life is empty and sterile without her lover, who is not likely to come back to her, becomes so clear in it. There is no solution to her personal dilemma arousing suicidal thoughts in her. The lover whose company erstwhile enabled her to derive the utmost joy is lost for ever for her, while the licit source is sluggish and unsympathetic. It is a hellish life for a domestic woman, to which the opening lines of the poem point out.

Very often in her poetry Kamala Das identifies the 'sea' with the source of solace and comfort and redemption, whereas the 'heat' or the 'sun' connotes the opposite forces of oppression and exploitation (as specially to be witnessed in the domineering male tyranny). Here also the poetess looks to the sea as usual and eventually accepts its invitation of self-drowning — 'Darling forgive, how long can one resist?' (*The Decendants*, p. 15). In *My Story*, she writes in one place: "Often I have toyed with the idea of drowning myself to be rid of my loneliness which is not unique in any way but is natural to all. I have wanted to find rest in the sea and an escape from involvements."[7] Commenting on this poem, Devinder Kohli observes: "Kamala Das is not romanticising death by comparing it to the ecstasy of love, but by approaching the language of delirium suggests the feeling of torture that seems to accompany her more recent treatment of sexual love. This is perhaps unconscious...."[8]

*Clenching, unclenching* — closing in and opening of fists.

*garrulous* — talkative, loquacious.

*slosh up* — stir or splash upward.

*Slide down* — slip down gently.

*anemones* — a kind of sea-plants.

7. *My Story*, p. 227.
8. Kohli, *op. cit.*, p. 90.

*inert* — slow, sluggish.
*blotted* — wiped out.
*whiplash* — whipbeating.
*prying* — looking furtively at, watching something secretly,

**(f) The Looking Glass**

This poem is also culled from *The Descendants* (1967). Like "Ferns" and "Convicts" in this volume, it is about physical love between a man and a woman. It is "both patronizing and indulgent in tone." The woman in it is every woman that seeks love, and the man is every man that wants a woman to satisfy his sex-hunger. The poem faithfully reflects the mutual need of man and woman for physical enjoyment, and a woman must be truthful to this need of hers.

According to the poetess, a woman should be honest about her wants and requirements, and then it would be easy for her to get a man to love her. For physical gratification, she should draw close to him. She should not hesitate to stand naked before the looking-glass with him so that he sees it clearly that that he is stronger and she is weaker, younger, and lovelier. This will satisfy his male ego and excite his passion for the weaker sex. She should also accept his praise of her beauty and youth. In order to satisfy his male ego, she should point out to him that he is bodily perfect, and notice that his eyes are getting red in passionate excitement. She should also mark his shy walk across the bathroom floor, covering himself in a towel, and his jerky way of urination. She should, in short, admire him for all his good points and let him feel that he is her 'only man' for sexual satisfaction.

As a woman true to her nature, she should give herself over to him totally. She should offer to him the scent of her long hair, the musk of her breasts, and the warm shock of her menstrual blood. She should allow him to have his fill of sexual pleasure and indulge in it with all her 'endless female hungers.' He would then feel that she is not only satisfying his lust, but also hers.

Again, the poetess returns to the initial impulse in the poem, and asserts that it is easy to get a man to love a woman, but that it is very difficult so carry on her life after he has gone away for ever. For him, it is simply a sexual encounter with a lustful woman, but for her it entails all difficulties and tensions. On his desertion, she feels totally stranded in life, suffering humiliations and miseries of a forlorn woman. She was once in quest of emotional fulfilment, but she received only tears and sobs, in coming into contact with 'strangers.' Her body, which once gleamed under his touch like burnished brass, becomes now 'drab and destitute.' She is no more than a melancholy woman having onslaughts of disease and decay and deformity.

Speaking of this poem, M.L. Sharma writes as follows: "In this poem the poet offers a cool, almost a cold blooded, dispassionate and clinical analysis of the different stages of falling in love, the Machiavellian strategies to hold that love and the inevitable decline and fall of the heart's empire. The title of the poem could better have been 'Love's Progress.'" And further: "I find that the poem partakes of the maturer attitude of W.B. Yeats, when he was at once in love, to be passionately gripped by its storms, and out of it to take a cool clinical stock of the whole situation. The poem does not merely celebrate the passions of love; it simultaneously views the climax and the anti-climax through a bifocal vision which renders the complexity, ambivalence and the irony of the total situation in a much greater depth than is normally available to the Newtonian 'Single Vision', to adopt a Blakean phrase."[9]

The poem is simple and straightforward in its diction. It is highly charged with pulse and power. Passion seems to leap out of every line. A sharp feminine sensibility is at work here. As a full-blooded woman, Kamala Das makes an honest confession of her wants for her sexual gratification. The poem is decidedly a psychic striptease. It powerfully evokes the image of a lustful relationship between the two sexes. Nothing is, in truth, concealed from the reader, not even the ugly and the forbidden. There is a subtle psychological analysis of the male mentality in the first part of the poem, just as the second part is totally pervaded by a feminine consciousness. The cumulative effect of the poem is one of sterility and futility of sexual love.

*Admit your/Admiration* — The woman should accept her man's praise of her beauty and youth.

*eyes reddening under/Shower* — It is a beautiful image indeed, and suggests sexual consummation.

(Mark the word 'Shower' in this context).

*fond* — tender, sweet.

*the musk* — the scent obtained from the gland of musk-deer.

*A living without life* — a life without true love.

*gleamed* — shone slightly or momentarily.

*burnished* — polished; made bright by rubbing.

*now drab and destitute* — now dull and miserable.

---

9. *Kamala Das*, pp. 23-24.

## (g) The Old Playhouse

This is the title-piece of Kamala Das's third volume of verse, *The Old Playhouse and Other Poems* (1973). It is addressed to 'you,' to the husband, who wanted to curtail her freedom of movement and action through his subtle manoeuvrings. The poetic persona does not like this, just as she does not like him or his ways. His 'monstrous ego' comes under fire herein, since it has totally reduced her and disappointed her. As a result, her mind becomes 'an old playhouse with all lights put out.'

The poem, which was first published in *The Illustrated Weekly of India*, is a strong indictment against injurious male behaviour. It protests against the manner of treatment meted out to her by her own man. In *My Story*, it preludes Chapter 43 — "I too tried adultery for a short while." Obviously, it is an attempt to shatter all conventional and imposed bonds, including that of wedlock, upon a woman who craves for emotional fulfilment and sense of security. In the above-noted chapter of her autobiography, Kamala writes thus:

> Like the majority of city-dwelling women, I too tried adultery for a short while, but I found it distasteful. My lover had entered the decline of his career and aroused in me, more than love, a strong sense of pity.

and again as under:

> Years after all of it had ended, I asked myself why I took him on as my lover fully aware of his incapacity to love and I groped in my mind for the right answers. Love has a beginning and an end, but lust has no such faults. I needed security, I needed permanence, I needed two strong arms thrown around my shoulders and a soft voice in my ear. Physical integrity must carry with it a certain pride that is burden to the soul. Perhaps it was necessary for my body to defile itself in many ways, so that the soul turned humble for a change.[10]

These autobiographical extracts demonstrate clearly that the poetess needed love and tenderness, security and permanence, from her strong man, but he could not satisfy her on these scores. Hence her unredeemed damnation and suffering in his company.

The possessive instinct of the man is stressed in the opening of the poem. The man (or better, the poetess's husband) tried to tame a free bird that she was and subject her to sexual torture so that she should forget her happy seasons, old homes, and her intrinsic value as a woman. But she had come to him not to learn of him but of herself, and thereby

10. *My Story*, pp. 193-94.

'grow' in a carefree atmosphere. He was pleased with her body's response and its fragile convulsions. He made hectic love to her and overwhelmed her by his forceful physical contact. He rather overflooded the organs of her body by an energetic mating and dribbled his spittle into her mouth. He called her 'wife,' who was taught to attend to her domestic duties ungrudgingly and look after him properly by supplying him tea, food and vitamins at the needed moments. She tried to adjust herself in accordance with his wishes, but she lost her individuality in the process and became a mere dwarf under his disastrous male ego. She was totally reduced and annihilated in due course:

> Cowering
> beneath your monstrous ego I ate the magic loaf and
> Became a dwarf. I lost my will and reason, to all your
> Questions I mumbled incoherent replies.

The days of happiness came to a grinding halt in her case, — 'The summer/Begins to pall.' She began to feel the arrival of the autumn for her and the suffocating atmosphere of the burning leaves and the rising smoke. The man she loved adopts artificial measures to satisfy himself — 'artificial lights' — and grows indifferent and insolent towards her by keeping his windows shut. But the artificial measures have not helped him in any way to override his dominating male impulse. Even his 'breath' is strongly masculine. The overall impact of all this on her is dejection and cheerlessness, with no hope of regeneration. Her singing is gone, her dance is forsaken, and her mind becomes 'an old playhouse with all its lights put out.' As contrasted to this, the man adopts a hard line towards her, and serves his love in deadly doses, whereas for her love is self-obsessed and unenjoy able, and yet it seeks its fulfilment in freedom rather than in bondage. Love for its healthy growth wants to be pure and emotional, and not lustful and muddy (as the poetess's husband doles out for her). The expressions like 'the water's edge' and 'to erase the water' signify sexual consummation between the man and the woman, which the woman-persona does not like.

In this poem, the poetess's personal predicament is aired out. She who was as free as a swallow has now been domesticated with all her wings severed. She desired to discover a meaning, a perfect fulfilment through love, but her man broke her completely by thrusting household responsibilities on her shoulders and by creating barricades for her in life. He asserted his marital prerogatives, curtailed her freedom totally, showed his masculine power to her. Consequently, she became a dwarf under the heavy weight of his lustful masculinity and monstrous ego. All her hopes were dashed into pieces; all her cheerful spirits disappeared for good. She began to feel a great emotional vacuum, and couldn't enjoy sexual encounters with him. She got possessed with an abnormal psychology and sought love at strangers' doors. The lustful advance of her man grew distasteful to her and she took revenge upon him by craving for freedom from his snares and by seeking shelter in others' arms (to use her own expression).

In its tone and temper, the poem is gloomy and pessimistic. In its language, it is fiery and charged. At places it gives the impression of being verbose and long-winded. The metaphorical expression — 'my mind is an old/Playhouse with all its lights put out' (p. 1) — is highly impressive and truculent. There are difficult words used here and there in the poem, but the meaning is quite plain everywhere. The central idea is 'freedom.' The woman was free as a swallow in the beginning, and she aspires for freedom in the end:

> ...and yet it must seek at last
> An end, a pure, total freedom.... (pp. 1-2).

The middle of the poem strikes the note of paradox in her situation; her 'freedom' so long cherished and so highly valued is completely curtailed and her personality totally annihilated. She had never dreamt of it, and when it stood as a reality before her she was terribly shocked, she felt utterly lonely and miserable.

*You planned to tame a swallow* — An address to her husband, who attempted to domesticate her and curtail her freedom.

*Lesson...about yourself* — This gives us an idea of the highly egotistic nature of her husband.

*its usual.../Convulsions* — the body's vibrations to his sexual assaults.

*dribbled spittle* — The husband let his sputum roll into her mouth; — a distasteful thing indeed.

*every nook and cranny* — every comer and small opening.

*embalmed* — preserved something (usually a corpse) from decay.

*saccharine* — extremely sweet substance from coal-tar.

*a dwarf* — an unusually small person.

*I mumbled*...replies — I gave indistinct and inconsistent answers.

*to pall* — to become tasteless or tiresome, the fall — the autumn.

*the vases* — the jars for holding flowers for decoration.

*lethal* — deadly, fatal.

*Narcissus* — A youth in Classical Mythology who fell in love with his own image reflected in a pool and wasted away from unsatisfied desire, whereupon he was transformed into a flower.

*the water* — It symbolises the sexual consummation when the lovers get saturated.

### (h) An Introduction

This poem first appeared in *Summer in Calcutta* and then in *The Old Playhouse and Other Poems.* It is one of the best poems ever written by Kamala Das. It is highly revealing of the poetess — of her political knowledge, of her linguistic acquirements, of her physical growth and marriage, of her sad experiences in married life, of her belongingness, of her love to another man, and of her eventual frustration and loneliness. It is definitely cast in a 'confessional' mode.

Introducing herself to her readers, the poetess tells them that she does not know politics, but she knows the names of influential, powerful persons, beginning with Nehru; that she is an Indian, very dark, born in Malabar, that she speaks three languages, writes in two, and dreams in one; that she writes in English despite objections from certain people and quarters, and that she has a strong claim to it; that English comes to her as naturally as cawing to the crows or roaring to the lions, and that it is competent to convey her emotions and thoughts; that she was married to a youth of sixteen when she grew up a little; that her husband did not beat her, but left her woman-persona crushed and broken; that she disliked him since then; that she started moving about in society in a male dress, ignoring her womanliness; that people again objected to it and wanted her to 'fit in' or 'belong' and not play pretending games or roles; that she, thereafter, fell in love with a man who also loved her; and that ultimately she drank deep at the well of pessimism and dispiritedness. This is all that she reveals about herself.

The tone of the poem is intimate and convincing; the language is simple yet sweeping. The swift movement of the lines is evident in its use of monosyllabism; for example, as in the following:

Dress in sarees, be girl,
Be wife, they said. Be embroiderer, be cook,
Be a quarreller with servants. Fit in. Oh,
Belong.... ... ... Don't sit
On walls or peep in through our lace-draped windows.
Be Amy, or be Kamala. Or, better

Still, be Madhavikutty. It is time to
Choose a name, a role.

(*The Old Playhouse...*, p. 27).

It is very rhythmical, and towards the close becomes incantatory. In it the poetess identifies herself with 'every woman' who seeks love. Prof. K.R.S. Iyengar characterizes this piece as "confessional."[11] And Devinder Kohli remarks about it thus: "An Introduction' is not only a candid and witty piece of self-revelation, but a state of her credo, her attitude to language and experience."[12]

*its queernesses* — its odds.

*the blazing...pyre* — It evokes the image of death and destruction.

*schizophrenia* — mental disorder with split personality.

*Nympho* — a woman with morbid sexual desire.

*Jilted* — cast off (in love), rejected, put aside.

11. *Indian Writing in English*, (1973), p. 678.
12. *Kamala Das* (1975), p. 83.

# 10

# Conclusion: As a Poetic Artist

Kamala Das, who took the literary world by storm in the mid-sixties, has created a permanent place for herself in contemporary Indo-English poetry. Though she has produced only three volumes of verse to date, which is a clear indication of her poetic energies getting dried up to some extent, she has been one of the most popular poets of India who have gained ground even in the West. And such Indian poets are not too many; in fact, they can be easily counted, A.K. Ramanujan, Dom Moraes, Nissim Ezekiel, Pritish Nandy, K.N. Daruwalla, Shiv K. Kumar, and herself. It is not, therefore, surprising that the noted English poet, Geoffrey Hill, was prompted to remark that the one poet who stood out in P. Lal's *Modern Indian Poetry in English: An Anthology and a Credo* (1969) was Kamala Das. In points of enjoyment and applause, she stands next to none in the whole length and breadth of Indian poetry in English today.

Kamala Das as a poet treads on familiar grounds, and she never tries to transgress her self-imposed restrictions. She is, after all, a woman with a narrow range of experience in life, but she makes the best of the crippling situations around. In this context, she reminds us of another woman writer, Jane Austen, who is so well-known for her 'two inches of ivory.' Like Austen, Kamala Das also moves within her limited range with grace and skill. The advantage of this range is that it offers to the reader only what the writer has personally felt and realised, and nothing borrowed from another source.

As a poet of sharp feminine sensibility, Kamala Das gives vent to the hopes, fears and desires of womankind. She has been the champion of woman's cause in all her writings, and there is no point in challenging this statement which amounts to an altruism. In a seminar held in Lucknow in December 1980, I was questioned on the proposition that there is a 'feminine sensibility at work' in her poetry. I am still convinced that this sensibility is amply in evidence in her work, and no frivolous argument against such a self-evident truth can dislodge me from my stand. Now, what can one say about such lines as the following?

Love is not important, that makes the blood
Carouse, nor the man who brands you with his
Lust, but is shed as slough at end of each
Embrace. Only that matters which forms as
Toadstool under lightning and rain, the soft
Stir in womb, the foetus growing, for,
Only the treasures matter that were washed
Ashore, not the long blue tides that washed them
In.

("Jaisurya")

This comes from a sensitive woman having experienced maternity and throes of delivery. Kamala Das's poems like "A Relationship," "*Summer in Calcutta*," "An Introduction," "Marine Drive," and several others bring to the fore her boldness and freedom in speaking aloud the secret longings and aspirations of womankind. The following extract from "*Summer in Calcutta*" is inspired by a woman's hectic search for the desired love under the scorching sun:

My worries
Doze. Wee bubbles ring
My glass, like a bride's
Nervous smile, and meet
My lips. Dear, forgive
This moment's lull in
Wanting you, the blur
In memory.

Not only in her poetry, but also in her essays Kamala Das comes out as an unofficial spokesman of the Indian counterpart of the woman's 'Tib' movement in the West, and her essays like "Why Not More Than One Husband?" "What Women Expect Out of Marriage And What They Get," and "The She-Mouse Returns Home" bear it out.

But Kamala Das can't be as emancipated as Germaine Greer, or as wild as Tennyson's Princess (in the poem of that name), or as socially active as Sarojini Naidu, to do away with the injustices meted out to womankind, and she readily accepts the limitations of a family life. In this connection, she is comparable to the well-known Australian poet, Judith Wright, who too sees the experience of love ennobled in marriage and family rather than degraded in any way. In Kamala Das we find much that is conventional and feminine, and she speaks aloud the needs find fears of a common woman and pleads for authentic love and sense of security for her out of her own knowledge. And yet, the woman in her cannot be completely shadowed, and so she cannot help expressing an ambivalence proceeding from her own duality, from the combination in herself of a need for domestic security and the inborn desire to be liberated. As we know she was married at an early age and she did not find her married life altogether happy or satisfactory (as the tone of her poems suggests and as reaffirmed by her autobiography, *My Story*), and so her life-story, notwithstanding its sensationalism which seems to be partly contrived, makes a poignant reading. Marriage and love forming the dominant theme of Mrs. Das's poetry need not be mutually exclusive, but for her it has invariably proved to be so. When she speaks of love outside marriage, she does not necessarily propagate the institution of adultery or infidelity, but seems to be merely searching for a relationship which gives both genuine love and impenetrable security. That's why she sometimes gives a mythical framework to her search for true love, and identifies it with the Radha-Krishna syndrome or with that of Mira Bai relinquishing the ties of marriage in pursuit of Lord Krishna, the true divine lover:

> Vrindavan lives on in every woman's mind,
> and the flute, luring her
> From home and her husband
> Who later asks her of the long scratch on the brown
> Aureola of her breast, and she shyly replies,
> hiding flushed cheeks,
> It was so dark outside, I tripped and fell over
> the brambles in the wood....

The poem "Ghanshyam" is a relevant example in this context. Like Sarojini Naidu in her poem on Ghanshyam, Kamala Das ventilates her mystical longings and mythical leanings in this beautiful piece.

Kamala Das is primarily a poet of love. Evidently, she is not so much preoccupied with a metaphysical quest or with a formulation of poetic theory as with an intense search for love. In a letter to Devinder Kohli dated 10th December 1968, she admits that 'I began to write poetry with the ignoble aim of wooing a man. There is therefore a lot of love in my poems,' and that the poems contained in *Summer in Calcutta* were composed with the sole objective of making 'a man love me' and of 'breaking down his resistance.'[1] As a poet of love, Kamala Das looks most naive, honest, and frank, almost in the fashion of Sappho, though she does not possess the 'intellectual pride' and the 'open-hearted ease' of Judith Wright. But it must also be mentioned here that Kamala wrote her poetry against a conservative and tabooed society, and not against a free and uninhibited society of Australia, and this accounts for the difference between the two celebrated poetesses. As compared to some other women-poets of the confessional mode (which is definitely Kamala's due by all means), such as Anne Saxton and Sylvia Plath, Kamala Das may fall short of intellectual vigour and witty tit-bits, but she does not lag behind in lyrical outburst of unpremeditated thoughts and feelings and in emotional intensity. In truth, she is more aware of the pathos in the life of a common woman playing a very passive role in our tradition-bound society than some of these women poets highlighting a different cultural and moral ethos. And how bold and courageous is this lady of our land may be clearly judged from the fact that she articulates the theme of sexual love in such a frank manner that we are left wonderstmck at it. There is an air of unconventionality about it.

Related to the theme of lovc is the celebration of the 'body' in Kamala Das's poetry. This celebration is not in the style of Gieve Patel who makes a clinical analysis of the body in a general way. Kamala's approach is perfectly personal, adding a touch of delicacy and charm to it. Her poems indicate that she both likes and dislikes her body. Physically she is dark-complexioned with 'ordinary features,' and her loathing for the body is partly due to this and partly due to her protracted illnesses. In liking the body, she is led by the pleasures it affords to her and to her companion. In this matter, she resembles another distinguished Indo-English poet, Nissim Ezekiel, who is also a 'poet of the body.' In case of Kamala Das, the tensions actually issue forth from the pressures of her complex family background, — neither she was properly cared for by her parents, nor by her office-going husband after her marriage. This is how she conveys her feelings at her parental and husband's homes:

> I was a burden and a responsibility neither my parents nor my grandfather could put up with for long. Therefore with the blessings of all, our marriage was fixed.[2]

1. See D. Kohli's book, *Kamala Das*, pp. 29 and 58 respectively.
2. Kamala Das, *My Story*, p. 85.

and:

> My husband was immersed in his office-work, and after work there was the dinner, followed by sex. Where was there any time left for him to want to see the sea or dark buffaloes of the slopes?[3]

Evidently, the failure of love and the birth of poetry seem to be related to each other in Mrs. Das. Her poems like "The Suicide," The Prisoner," and "Advice to Fellow Swimmers" are the glaring examples of it. This is what she says in "The Prisoner":

As the convict studies
His prison's geography
I study the trappings
Of your body, dear love,
For I must someday find
An escape from its snare.

In singing of the body, she finds no true love from her legitimate source and she tells us that her intimacy with her husband was 'purely physical.' Under such circumstances, love degenerates into lust, loud and savage, with which she is fed up in her life, and she makes a fervent appeal to her readers:

When I die
Do not throw
The meat and bones away
But pile them up
And let them tell
By their smell
What life was worth
On this earth
What love was worth
In the end.

The naked body became more acceptable to her during her illness than in her normal health, and she has spoken of this in one of the excerpts of her best-selling autobiography:

> Whenever he tried to strip me of my clothes, my shyness clung to me like a second skin and made my movements graceless. Each pore of my skin became at that moment a seeing eye, an eye that viewed my body with distaste. But

3. Kamala Das, "I Have Lived Beautifully," *Debonair*, III, No. 5 (May 15, 1975), p. 41.

> during my illness, I shed my shyness and for the first time
> in my life learned to surrender totally in bed with my pride
> intact and blazing.[4]

Perhaps in the moments of her convalescence, she needed her man's tenderness and reassuring love, which she accepted most heartily.

Kamala Das is a poet not so much of the countryside as of the city. In this regard, she is like most of Indo-English poets, for, in the words of Gauri Deslfpande, there is "nothing...pastoral or rural in the preoccupations of these poets,"[5] and this is a failure of Indian poetry in English in general. As a result, Nature that formed so great a stimulus in the writings of the English Romantic poets is almost completely banished from its domain. K.N. Daruwalla with his powerful rural paintings is one obvious exception, and his poems like "In the Tarai," "The Ghaghra in Spate," "Haranag," "Boat-ride along the Ganges," and many others testify to this truth. In the second-named poem, we have:

> And through the village
> the Ghaghra steers her course:
> thatch and dung-cakes turn to river-scum,
> a buffalo floats over to the rooftop
> where the men are stranded.
> Three days of hunger, and her udders
> turn red-rimmed and swollen
> with milk-extortion.

Now, if one looks for such poems in Kamala Das, one will be disappointed. But she is not totally ignorant about lively Nature; after all she knows the sea and the sea-waters very well, and they also figure in her verse. She also deplores her moving away from the sights and sounds of the idyllic countryside surrounding her parental house to the 'dusty cities' with their din and disturbance. Like Nissim Ezekiel, she depicts the squalor and the heat, the crowd and the slum-life, with a precision marked with reality that is really enviable, and at the same time she remains true to her experience and realisation without being over-idealistic or cynical like the Romantics. Her first volume, in particular, strikes a remarkable harmony between her private, burning passion and the dazzling, scorching sunlight. And this she achieves without taking recourse to the biting social irony of Nissim Ezekiel or savage subjective irony of Shiv K.

---

4. *My Story*, p. 118.
5. G. Deshpande, "Foreword", *An Anthology of Indo-English Poetry* (Delhi: Hind Pocket Books, n.d.), p. 12.

Kumar, and she is certainly not alienated from her social milieu as Dom Moraes, for instance, is.

As a poet of the city, Kamala Das constantly employs the metaphor of the city for life, such as in the poem "A New City." There is an anguished awareness on the part of the poetess to have lost something in adopting the city as her home, but she is also aware of the joys and amenities to be found in a city. Thus, she discovers that 'all the Delhi streets' are 'fragrant and murky' rendering her 'very young, very lovely and delightfully carefree.'

Elsewhere, she contrasts the inviolable peace of the Delhi landscape with the disturbed mind of the poet. She bids a touching farewell to the city of her long residence, Bombay, which she loves so deeply:

I take leave of you, fair city, while tears
Hide somewhere in my adult eyes
And sadness is silent as a stone
In the river's unmoving
Core...
It's goodbye, goodbye, goodbye,
To slender shapes behind windowpanes,
Shut against indiscriminate desire
And rain....

This departure is as painful as the parting of a loved one, as the city forms an integral part of the emotional make-up of the poet.

The later poetry of Kamala Das shows her intense concern with death and decay in human life, and the element of 'discontentment' is pervasive in it. The poem "Lines to a Husband" contains two parallel strands in it — the obsession with physical decay and destruction, and the obsession with love which remains unrequited in her life. And the poem "The Suicide" moves a step ahead in visualising not only the death of the body but also of the soul. Here she writes:

Bereft of soul
My body shall be bare.
Bereft of body
My soul shall be bare.
Which would you rather have
O kind sea?

and further:

O sea, I am fed up
I want to be simple

I want to be loved
And
If love is not to be had
I want to be dead, just dead
While I enter deeper....

Out of deep anguish, she cries out in another poem:

From the debris of housewrecks
Pick up my broken face,
Your bride's face,
Changed a little with the years.
I shall not remember
The betrayed honeymoon;
We are both such cynics,
You and I.

The poem "The Sorcerers and Exorcists of Kattumadam" informs us that the poet suffered a nervous breakdown at the age of nineteen as a 'neglected wife' and a stay in Malabar with her loved grandmother could cure her. For a different reason, Sylvia Plath also had suffered a similar nervous breakdown almost at the same age, — that was due to an intense, nearly unbearable, love for her adored father. But whereas Kamala could be cured, Sylvia could not be.

One of the central characters in Kamala Das's work is her grandmother who is inseparably linked with her memory of the parental home now more than three hundred years old. Here she felt at home, and got her diseases cured. She describes it as 'a paradise on earth for me.' In "My Grandmother's House" (*Summer in Calcutta*), she celebrates this house as the seat of her great comfort and abounding in love and life:

There is a house now far away where once
I received love... That woman died,
The house withdrew into silence, snakes moved
Among books I was then too young
To read, and my blood turned cold like the moon
How often I think of going
There....

The poem "Blood" is an apotheosis of the house — 'this old house beside the sea' — as well as of the grandmother. Mrs. Das's fascination with the images of the old house besides the beating sea can be clearly traced back to her childhood associations with it. We know, A.K. Ramanujan also delineates his impressions about his parental house in his well-known poem "Small-Scale Reflections on a Great House," but here Ramanujan's attitude is unmistakably ironic, whereas Kamala Das's attitude remains reverential and affectionate throughout.

In Kamala Das's poetry one comes across the intensity of passions which renders words irrelevant for articulation. Obviously, silence and not words is the tree language of love, and Kamala Das shows her distaste for the abstract and her preference for the elemental by laying stress on the role of silence as a dramatic device in a poem charged with pulse and power. She cannot say, like Yeats, that 'words alone are certain good,' or as Nissim Ezekiel says that 'the best poets wait for words.' Though Kamala is conscious of the fact that words 'grow on me like leaves,' she knows well that they can ever play their semantic mischiefs and thus be a 'nuisance':

...beware of them, they
Can be so many things, a
Chasm where running feet must pause, to
Look, a sea with paralysing waves,
A blast of burning air or
A knife most willing to cut your best
Friend's throat .......

The poem "Substitute" suggests that words are a source of discord and disharmony after love-making. In another piece, "Convicts," words are submerged in the dark of passions and the music of silence, and Kamala Das writes:

When he
And I were one, we were neither
Male nor female. There were no more
Words left, all words lay imprisoned
In the ageing arms of night. In
Darkness we grew as in silence
We sang....

The lack of words does not, in any way, create the impression of inadequacy; it rather produces the desired effect of haste and urgency, especially so in Mrs. Das's poetry. She once observed, 'I like poetry to be disciplined and tidy'. But she feels the words are merely a medium of expression, and as such they should not be allowed to be treated as an absolute truth per se. As words are the products of conscious selection or rejection of the writer, they are usually opposed to the essential need of expressing the dark side of passion or the onrush of intense feelings. In her poetry Kamala Das shows the inadequacy of language to cope with the heavy weight of experiential records. Even a poet like T.S. Eliot, who has been a conscious artist throughout, is also preoccupied with this problem when he remarks that 'words' reach 'Word' and are, thereafter, heard no more, and he too treats them as a means of approaching the Eternity.

Gauri Deshpande, a reputed poet herself, brackets Kamala Das with Nissim Ezekiel for "the deft touch in the medium."[6] No doubt, her control over the medium of expression is almost sure and sound, but sometimes it slips off lamentably, giving the impression of a weak and self-indulgent writing. Occasionally she also indulges in repetitions of words, lines and even sections of a poem. This device has been used by D.H. Lawrence, Dylan Thomas, and the Bible, but Kamala Das does not satisfy us on this score. This is what we find in "The Testing of Sirens":

> Ah, why does love come to me like pain
> Again and again and again?

This tendency of the poet is also amply evident in her poem "Substitute," wherein she says:

> It will be all right when I learn
> To paint my mouth like a clown's.
> It will be all right if I put up my hair,
> Stand near my husband to make a proud pair.
> It will be all right if I join clubs
> And flirt a little over telephone.
> It will be all right, it will be all right
> I am the type that endures.
> It will be all right, it will be all right
> It will be all right between the world and me.
> It will be all right if I don't remember
> The last of the days together....

Here the repetition is made so unnerving that the reader gets almost bored and uninterested. Writing for *Quest* in April-June 1966 (p. 38), Linda Hess also remarked thus:

> There are major weaknesses in Mrs. Das's book.
> These can be characterized as a general carelessness in composition, a looseness typified by the alarming number of ellipses, three lazy dots thrown in at the end or middle of a line and seeming to say, 'This matter could be elaborated much further, but I lack either the wit or the energy to do it.' There are frequent repetitions of words and phrases, another quick solution to the problem of filling

6. G. Deshpande, *op. cit.*, p. 14.

> up a line but one that has disastrous effects on intensity and precision. There are patches of triteness and lapses of balance. Too often the end of a line brings an unnatural break in the diction which seems to have no excuse except the whim of the author.

Sometimes Kamala sounds theatrical in her verse, as in the poem "A Request," wherein she is busy visualising, like Thomas Hardy in his "Afterwards," what people should do with her after her death. She actually lacks the sense of proportion in her poetry, — that is, she does not know where to stop in the hurried mood of urgent expression. But a good poet (of her stature) must know it. The last thing to be said against her is that meie salubrious details of love and sex will not convince the reader about the fecundity of her imagination or about the continuity of her creativity. For one thing, she has produced no poetical volume independently since 1973.

When all her weaknesses have been pointed out, it remains to be observed here that Kamala Das in her best poems moves us deeply through her "passionate urge and drive of the rhythm" and through her "haunting images of sterility."[7] The poem "The Looking-Glass" is to be specially marked for its honesty and openness in the expression of a woman's inner thoughts of love and sex. Here she says:

> Getting a man to love you is easy
> Only be honest about your wants as
> Woman. Stand nude before the glass with him
> So that he sees himself the stronger one
> And believes it so, and you so much more
> Softer, younger, lovelier...Admit your Admiration.

This is a very fine example of her 'passionate urge' for making love to the man of one's desire. For the drive of her rhythm, one may quote a poem like "The Invitation," where she writes:

> I have a man's fist in my head today
> Clenching, unclenching....
> I have got all the Sunday evening pains.
> The sea is garrulous today. Come in,
> Come in. What do you lose by dying, and
> Besides, your losses are my gains.
> Oh Sea, let me. Shrink or grow, slosh up,
> Slide down, go your way,
> I will go mine.

---

7. Eunice de Souza, "Kamala Das, Gauri Deshpande, Mamta Kalia," *Contemporary Indian Poetry in English*, ed. Saleem Peeradina, p. 86.

The lines are almost even here, but the employment of monosyllabic or short words produces a tilting cadence in this piece, especially in the second and third stanzas. The poem "An Introduction," which is a brief autobiography of the poet, has the rhythms of conversational speech:

> Be Amy, or be Kamala. Or better
> Still, be Madhavikutty. It is time to
> Choose a name, a role. Don't play pretending games

"The Wild Bougainvillea" is another poem remarkable for its beauty and charm of continuously alternating long and short lines:

> I walked, I saw and
> I heard, the city tamed
> Itself for me, and then my hunger for a
> Particular touch waned
> And one day I sent him some roses and slept
> Through the night, a silent
> Dreamless sleep and woke up in the morning, free.

While there is not much of symbolism in Mrs. Das's poetry (as one surely finds in Sri Aurobindo's work), some arresting images are to be witnessed in it. These images make her verse really delightful, graphic, and pictorial. In this connection, we may cite "The Stone Age" as an illustration:

> Fond husband, ancient settler in the mind,
> Old fat spider, weaving webs of bewilderment,
> Be kind. You turn me into a bird of stone, a granite
> Dove ...................................
> ...With loud talk you bruise my pre-morning sleep,
> You stick a finger into my dreaming eye. And
> Yet, on daydreams, strong men cast their shadows, they
> sink
> Like white suns in the swell of my Dravidian blood,
> Secretly flow the drains beneath sacred cities.
> When you leave, I drive my blue battered car
> Along the bluer sea.

The details offered here immediately evoke the picture of a sexually disconsolate wife getting enamoured of some other stronger men who come her way. Das's concrete and sensuous imagery recalls Keats to our minds. The following poetic passage will confirm the veracity of this statement:

> He talks, turning a sun-stained
> Cheek to me, his mouth, a dark
> Cavern, where stalactites of

> Uneven teeth gleam, his right
> Hand on my knee, while our minds
> Are willed to race towards love;
> But, they only wander, tripping
> Idly over puddles of
> Desire....

The 'desire' definitely gets kindled while going through it.

It is pertinent to talk here of Kamala Das's diction, which usually tends to be lyrical and musical. Simplicity is the hallmark of her language, and she does not indulge in unnecessary verbal jugglery or pedantry, as some Indo-English poets are prone to do. One does not smack of the impact of Hulme-Pound-Eliot coterie that so insistently pleased for 'variety' and 'complexity' in a literary work. T.S. Eliot once pronounced emphatically thus:

> Our civilization comprehends great variety and complexity, and this variety and complexity, playing upon a refined sensibility, must produce various and complex results. The poet must become more and more comprehensive, more allusive, more indirect, in order to force, to dislocate, if necessary, language into his meaning.[8]

Kamala Das does not bother about such things, and her only concern seems to be the urgency of expression uncloyed by any allusions or intricacies. Her poems exactly boil over; for instance, "The Freaks," "Convicts," "The Old Playhouse," and "The Looking-Glass." This is the truly charged diction of an intense love-making:

> That was the only kind of love,
> This hacking at each other's parts
> Like convicts hacking, breaking clods
> At noon. We were earth under hot
> Sun. There was burning in our
> Veins and the cool mountain nights did
> Nothing to lessen heat. When he
> And I were one, we were neither
> Male nor female.

The language grows fiery and flaming here, and the reader inescapably feels the burning of his/her body while poring over these lines. The kind of frankness we witness in Mrs. Das is hardly to be had in many women poets of India and abroad. Thus, in "Substitute," she tells us

---

8. T.S. Eliot, "The Metaphysical Poets", *Selected Essays*, p. 248.

rather cynically about her experience of love in a language suffused with warmth and worldliness:

> After that love became a swivel-door,
> When one went out, another came in.

Poets like Judith Wright and Anne Sexton would have loved and told candidly about it, but here is a poet who opens out her very heart, its bums and aches, in a highly lyrical and amorous language.

Kamala Das, with her three poetical collections, is quite secure in the realm of Indo-English verse. She may not have written much like Pritish Nandy or Nissim Ezekiel, like Monika Varma and Lila Ray among the Indian women writers, and she may also not be as witty or intellectual as some other Confessional poets of the world, or as some 'academic' Indian poets like Shiv K. Kumar and A.K. Ramanujan, but she excels them all in popularity and feminine sensitivity. She has her own range, her own cosy bower to relax in, and she moves therein with perfect ease and felicity. Explicitly, nuns and spinsters might seek reasons to attack her, but she is a poet who has the power to hold her readers spell-bound right from the start. Devinder Kohli is right in pointing out that there is "something in the tone and temper of Kamala Das's work which made one sit up from the very first poem."[9] Linda Hess, a ruthless critic of Mrs. Das, also concedes that "a genuine poetic talent is at work here."[10] And finally, we fully agree with the noted Indo-English poet, R. Parthasarathy, when he remarks that "Kamala Das impresses by being very much herself in her poems," and that her "tone is distinctively feminine."[11]

9. D. Kohli, *op. cit*, p. 25.
10. Linda Hess, *Quest* (April-June 1966), p. 38.
11. R. Parthasarathy, "Kamala Das," *Ten Twentieth-Century Indian Poets*, p. 22.

# Appendices

## Appendix A

## *Alphabet of Lust* (1976): An Appraisal

This is a novel all about lust and sex, — a theme valid enough for Kamala Das to handle adroitly. Dedicated to Jaisurya, the third son of the writer, and running into 148 pages, this Orient Paperback publication has unity of purpose and thought, a good deal of irony and concentration. How far sex can go to secure the pride of place is to be witnessed here. Obviously, it is a sizzling story of a beautiful woman, who is also a famous poetess, and her sexual surrender out of greed and ambition to some of the best-placed cabinet ministers in Delhi and her rise to power and pelf in an unimaginable manner.

Manasi, the protagonist of the novel, is married to Amol Mitra in a huff after the sudden and unexpected air-crash death of her fiance, the elder brother of Vijay Raje, by whom she has a child in her womb. Vijay Raje, a six years' junior to his elder brother, is in deep love with Manasi, and when he grows up into an adult he makes up his mind to seize political power and thereby win his love. Until Raje appears on the scene, the life for the Mitras is quite happy and carefree though not financially well-off. When he visits Manasi at her husband's after a lapse of two decades, he makes advances to her which she rebuffs scornfully. He goes away disappointed. Through the pull of Sadasivrao, an elderly but conscientious politician, Raje becomes a leader of youths and draws closer to the Prime Minister of the country. But afterwards, he elbows Sadasivrao out of the Central cabinet taking an undue advantage of the P.M.'s displeasure with the latter, and steps in his shoes. On becoming a minister, he grabs power and influence in the capital, and sends off an emissary in Krishnan to Manasi with a concrete proposal of allurement for her — that she should spend a week with him in the best hotel in Simla and get in return diamond earrings. Ambitious as she is, she accepts the offer. Prior to this, she has been awarded, through the advocacy of Raje to the P.M., the coveted Padmashri and a long citation for her enviable services to Literature, and she now thinks that she will be killing two birds with one stone. She will tell her husband that she is going to Delhi to receive her awards, and she will also take the trip to Simla in the company of Raje. She does so. In the meantime, the P.M. is drawn to Manasi, as she has been repeatedly praised by Raje, whose design apparently is to promote his beloved into the P.M.'s favour and be ever secure in his saddle. After spending a week in Simla with Raje, Manasi returns to Delhi and meets the P.M. at a dinner hosted by one of Raje's friends. The P.M. is left alone with her on the pretext of a severe headache, and she feels for him in his utter loneliness. And when he makes love to her, she does not resist it, since she has already decided to offer her body to him: "I rented out my body for a pair of diamond earrings. And hereafter for power I shall rent it out to the most influential tenant I can hope to get" (p. 41). Since then the P.M. meets her regularly and regales his life. Very tactfully Manasi is first made a member of the Rajya Sabha, then the Minister of Information and Broadcasting, and thereafter the Home Minister. Raje totally withdraws from her lest his boss be annoyed. She pays occasional visits to Bombay, but has no time to stay with her husband or to write letters to her only daughter, Supama, who is now 19 years old studying in a boarding school at Lucknow. On her birthday, she asks Raje, who is going to Lucknow on some official commission, to call on her daughter and present a parcel of gifts to her. Raje's rapacious eyes fall on the beaming beauty that Supama is and he invites her to a very good hotel in the city where he feeds her deliciously and tries to rape her then and there. Supama is dazed and stunned at this, and sobs continually in the night, and in the early morning catches a train for Bombay to reveal all this to her sincere boy-friend, Cyril Contractor. Sensing a sort of trouble for himself, Raje rushes to Bombay to calm her down. At her home she is all alone when he comes in, and she is greatly surprised to see him there. She tells him that she has not disclosed the matter to her parents nor has she any desire to do so. Raje again catches hold of her and begins caressing her temples, locks and breasts, at which she waxes extremely emotional and accepts his offer of Simla visit for a few days. He tells her:

> My darling girl, I cannot live without you...caressing her breasts and her arms. Come away with me this minute. Come to Simla. We, shall be happy together for a while.

> We shall get married. We shall be the happiest of married couples, (p. 126).

Together they go to the same hotel where earlier her mother had made love to him, to the same room and to the same bed. What an irony of situation! They make intense love to each other and decide to get married soon. Supama becomes pregnant too. When Manasi hears of this, she sadly repents her associations with Raje, and complains of it to the Prime Minister after revealing her daughter's identity — that she was Raje's own niece. The Prime Minister who had earlier wanted her daughter to marry Raje asks her to divulge the secrets to the latter. Supama is whisked away to Bombay in a plane and is taken to a clinic for termination of her pregnancy, but she manages to run away from there to Poona along with her boy-friend, Cyrus Contractor, a truly well-meaning person. By the time they are located by the police at Poona, they get married and obtain a certificate to the effect and settle in a hotel. Manasi, who is now the Home Minister and the right hand of the Prime Minister, rushes to Poona in the company of Raje and blesses the new-weds and persuades them to return to Bombay and live there in peace and happiness. Meanwhile, her private secretary informs her of the illness of the Prime Minister, and she with Raje leaves for Delhi in a helicopter to attend on him. The party elders and bosses had already agreed to her name as the next Prime Minister, and she has "nothing on her mind now except her long felt desire to be the head of the country" (p. 147). This is where the novel ends.

Parallel to this story of incest runs the sub-plot of political corruption rife in the government. On the death of the previous Prime Minister, the present one is installed in his place. A weak-kneed Prime Minister would be most acceptable to party bosses. The Prime Minister, Mr. Desai, who has a clean conscience, is somewhat irritable and short-tempered. He gets annoyed with Sadasivrao for no fault of his, rather for his frankness and honesty. But since Sadasivrao was a stumbling-block in the way of power-hungry Vijay Raje, the latter coaxed the Prime Minister to shunt the former out of the cabinet. Raje took over his post as a representative leader of the youths of the country. He starts spreading canards about the older politician, and engages men to hurl bombs at his public-meeting in Bombay, and when after a month's hospitalization he is to return home he visits him with a bouquet and conspires with one at the medical men to inject poison to him. As a result, Sadasivrao dies. Cyrus complains of it personally to the Prime Minister, but Raje grows dramatically ignorant about it, saying that the old man was like his father and had been his political mentor once upon a time. Raje was instrumental in getting his beloved, Manasi, elevated to the highest government post, though in the end he becomes jealous of her when she is selected as the Prime Minister of the country. Another instance of the political rot is that all the cabinet colleagues of the former P.M. are corrupt and blacklisted, and occasionally they cause pains and headaches to him. The Prime Minister is also not so pure — he is exposed to love and lust and Manasi is his weakness. He has picked up a wrong man — Vijay Raje — as his adviser. It may verily be said that Raje is the villain of the piece who is despicably black and wicked to the core (more details about him will follow).

To please the politicians, the industrialists and businessmen play a seductive role. Krishnan is one of them, collecting beautiful girls from all parts of the land who are offered to Raje to keep him in good cheers, or his permits and licences will stop. Krishnan was the person who had come to Manasi as a messenger of Raje. Later, he sends Stella, a deaf and mute inmate of an orphanage, to him. Similarly, Srinivasachari, the ageing chairman of a leading Public Sector undertaking, constantly encouraged by his mistress,

Anasuya Devi, who is Principal of the best women's college in Bombay, to trap Raje in by supplying the charming dancer, Sita, to him, otherwise he will lose his lucrative job.

Furthermore, the administrative class also comes under fire in this novel. Mihir Bandhopadhyay of the Indian Civil Service, who is hostile to the honest and hardworking Mitra, the husband of Manasi, tries to exploit the latter for his self-fulfilment. One has a very poor idea about the upper class and its sense of morality by reading this novel. This class is seen hatching plans to placate the corrupt politicians and the loose administrators, without ever attending to the call of conscience.

One single man rotten to the core is Vijay Raje. Initially, Manasi considered him as "a corrupt man, an astute manipulator" (p. 19), but later she fell a prey to his freakish love-offer. As she herself is greedy and ambitious, she accepts his invitation of going to Simla for a week and enjoy life there. What is most shocking in this novel is the seduction of Supama by him. Raje is an irresistible womaniser who resorts to all sorts of tricks and policies in trapping the fairer sex in his net. His repressed desire for women erupts with a volcanic fire, and he goes to any extent to procure them, so much so that he misuses his ministerial coat. He kills Stella, an orphan, for no fault of hers, and Krishnan is to blame for having sent her to him for a suitable job. Krishnan is another rogue in the novel who is a befitting companion for Raje. Srinivasachari and Anusuya Devi are fully aware of Raje's weakness for beautiful women, and hence they plan to send the charming Sita to him. Raje has apparently made sexual encounter with many a woman, and his so-called love is nothing but his lust which he tries to satiate by fair or foul means. Also, he is responsible for the exit of so many politicians and ministers, having set his eye on his own security. He is very clever and cunning in offering tactful and timely suggestions to the Prime Minister. He wants to put an end to all dissenting voices in his party, and does not hesitate to advise the Prime Minister to wage 'a fake war' with a neighbouring country in order to win the public opinion to their side and thereby succeed admirably in the next elections, otherwise people know it well that those who have the reins of the land in their hands are merely a pack of hounds, — a bunch of blacklisted, immoral politicians. To fulfil his aspiration of rising to the positions of power and pelf, he removes Sadasivrao from the scene for good. In short, he is a man who has no moral scruples whatsoever, though his accomplice, Krishnan, may prefer to call him "a saint" (p. 100) and "a man of great generosity" (p. 101).

The protagonist of the novel, Manasi, is a famous poetess of Bengal. She is young and beautiful, desired by some of the most influential politicians of the land. She was betrothed to Vijay's elder brother, who died in an air-crash, but before his death she had a brief love-affair with him. Consequently, she got pregnant, and when nobody accepted her for a wife, Amol Mitra, a struggling Government official who looked old enough to be her father, took her hand. This had made her a poetess, as the novelist suggests — "But then she would not have been a poetess, for her poetry had burst out of the mire of her utter hopelessness like a red lotus" (p. 9). Mitra was always honest and sincere in his dealings with her, and he never revealed her secret to anyone, not even during the moments of their strained relationship. She, too, was all happy and content until the appearance of Vijay Raje on the scene. Initially, she rebuffs Raje's advances towards her, but later when he becomes powerful politically as a youth leader and sends Krishnan to her with a tempting proposal of spending a week with him in the best hotel in Simla and get in return diamond earrings, she surrenders to him. She is also to blame, being very ambitious and power-hungry, and more than Raje it is her own inordinate desire that seduces her. She rises as a popular poetess, but her attitude of indifference towards her husband is hardly justifiable. This is what the novelist offers us about her character: "She felt pity for herself. She was still attractive. Her mind was active and very much alive. She was admired by the young as a revolutionary poetess. But her husband, the mild Mr. Mitra, had faded with the years, signing on millions of files, until he had become to her only a shabby appendage which she had to tote with her while she went to public function to preside" (p. 17). She actually repents to have married him: "She gave a rueful laugh. I am a sentimental ass, she told herself.

I shall never be able to leave him for any other man. If at all I marry again he will accompany me to my new home as part of my trousseau..." (pp. 17-18). No doubt, she finds 'any other man' in her hunt for lust and authority. The 'other man' she finds is Vijay Raje, who is equally rotten and evil-minded. Having accepted his offer once, there is no going back for her. She is introduced to the Prime Minister, who loves her to do away his loneliness. She likes it at the cost of her husband, her family, neglecting her school-going girl at Lucknow. The result is perilous. The family-life is totally disintegrated; Mitra gets resigned to his lot; Miss Supama, the daughter, follows in the footsteps of her mother, being trapped and ravished by the same Raje in the same hotel, nay in the same room and on the same bed, at Simla where he had once slept with Manasi. She herself knows that she has done a nasty thing, and she says to Vijay: "It is not as if I am a chaste woman now. *A pativrata*. You saw to it that I became a mere tart. I rented out my body for a pair of diamond earrings. And hereafter for power I shall rent it out to the most influential tenant I can hope to get" (p. 41). Thereafter, her torrid love-affairs with Raje and then with the Prime Minister become the talk of the townsfolk. She is awarded Padmashri; she is made a minister; she becomes 'a real bitch.' This is what the novelist gives us about her:

> Of course, her mother (Supama's mother), after joining politics, had turned into a real BITCH. She had cut her hair short and waved it carelessly in the Audrey Hepburn style. She took to smoking. Perhaps she had begun to drink too. She had certainly changed in her appearance. There were swellings under her eyes and an unhealthy flush on her cheeks. She had lost weight. She had picked up certain mannerisms which would have looked well in a lady like Miss Hepburn but was strange in a Bengali" woman who had been for two decades the reigning queen of the literary scene (p. 86).

But in her case 'character is destiny,' which recoils when Supama is raped by Raje. She now feels, Raje is an immoral man, who will never have the fruits of his misdeed. So, abortion is arranged for Supama. Manasi is elevated to the highest post of the Prime Minister. Though 'defeated' by

Raje in love-affairs and physical matters, she wreaks a revenge upon him by snatching away the Prime Ministership from him.

There are only two good and moral characters in the entire novel — Amol Mitra and Cyrus Contractor. They stand head and shoulders above others. Of these two, Mitra helps Manasi to get over her crisis at the beginning of her adult life, and Cyrus comes to the rescue of Supama when she is badly let down by Raje. Mitra is aged 56, but is pure and honest and hard-working. 'Kindness' is his virtue (p. 18). As a student, he had won a scholarship, but is presently satisfied with his official job as a clerk. Again and again, she is mentioned as docile and mild, 'modest and unassuming' (p. 110). He is tolerant and does not open his mouth to his superior officers even when he is humiliated. He is quick to perceive the blunders of Manasi, and points them out to her when once she comes home from Delhi for a while.

Cyrus Contractor is a young man of 24. He is bold and fearless by nature. When Sadasivrao is wounded terribly in a bomb-blast on the public platform, Cyrus arranges for his medical treatment in a nearby hospital. It was during his absence that Raje could have the old man killed by a poisonous injection. So courageous and resolute is he that he decides to expose Raje in the eyes of the Prime Minister. He goes to Delhi for this. The Prime Minister, who is sometimes pricked by his inner urges, asks Raje about the death of Sadasivrao. He angrily says: "Stop it, Raje, shouted the Prime Minister. You know well that he was murdered. Did you set someone to do it?" To this Raje replies thus: "Nonsense,... You are out of your mind today. Why should I get poor Sadasiv Chacha killed? He loved me like a son. It was on his knee that I picked up my political sense" (p. 128). Later Cyrus, who loves Supama from school days, comes to her help in hours of need. Not only he releases her from the snares of Raje, but also accepts her as his wife through court-marriage. Manasi is left with no option but to bless the two young loving hearts. In accepting Supama after her miserable condition, Cyrus once again shows exemplary courage. He does not bother about social customs and taboos.

There is also a whole set of minor characters in the novel. These characters are not fully developed, and they make their appearances in the text now and then to play subsidiary roles. They are like the contours of a picture. Of such characters, mention may be made of the Prime Minister Desai, Supama, Sadasivrao, Krishnan, Stella, Anasuya Devi, Srinivasachari, Mihir Bandhopadhyay, Sita, etc. The Prime Minister, Sadasivrao, and Supama are definitely creatures of flesh and blood, but others simply do not matter as they are merely 'pimps.' The P.M. is a man of conscience, while Sadasivrao an idealistic politician of the older generation. Supama is just a teenager bubbling with life and laughter until Raje comes into the picture and spoils her happiness and modesty.

To conclude, *Alphabet of Lust* is a titillating story of 'an ambitious woman's rise to power through sexual surrender' (to use the blurb matter). It is a powerful novel of 'lust' and illicit love, with Raje and Manasi at the helm of affairs. If Manasi is an embodiment of sexual debasement, Raje is that of political corruption. Both combine to give a brilliant flash to the social and political malaise in the Indian context. There are certain tmly tragic situations in this novel, such as the seduction of Supama by Raje, the killing of Stella by the same man, Manasi's negligence of her motherly duties towards Supama and her wifely duties towards Mitra, and Sadasivrao's untimely expiry, and these again conglomerate into the texture of the piece to render it highly readable and enjoyable. And since the novel spans within the experiences of its creator, it is definitely authentic and convincing.

# Appendix B

# The Other Harmony: Kamala Das's Prose

Scanty attention has been paid to Kamala Das as a writer of sparkling prose, whereas as a poetess she has been largely studied, commented on, and highlighted. Scholars who have studied her poetry[1] have generally by-passed her distinctive contribution to the other harmony, which is no less gripping and stimulating. The tragedy of Indian-English Criticism is that it shabbily runs after the select established authors, that it pursues a beaten track, and that it does not discover new areas of investigation in order to reveal the valuable hidden treasures therein. Though this is a sad reflection on our present-day critical business, it is a brazen reality that we will have to accept with heavy hearts. The lucky few like Rabindranath Tagore and Sri Aurobindo might have escaped its dreadful dragnet, but many other burgeoning and blooming creative talents have rightly suspected the proud "oblivion's curse," to borrow an expression from Torn Dutt.[2] In this connection, one need be reminded of famous poetic pronouncement of Thomas Gray — "Full many a flower is born to blush unseen."[3] But as a critic of Mrs. Das conscious of my literary responsibilities, I shall not let her down as a writer of English prose, and to accomplish my task through certain severe restrictions[4] I shall solely confine myself to her three prose works, namely *My Story* (1976),* *Alphabet of Lust* (1976),* and *A Doll for the Child Prostitute* (1977), which are presently available in book form.

## I

*My Story* had its genesis in one of the serious illnesses of Mrs. Das, as she herself informs us: "*My Story* is my autobiography which I began writing during my first serious bout with heart disease."[5] This autobiography was

* As this work has been studied in Appendix A, it will be left out.

begun to distract her mind from the fear of a sudden death as well as to clear her outstanding hospital bills. She wrote it through intermittent snatches of sleep and hybernations of the prescribed drugs. The impulse behind the work was, as she tells us, "to empty myself of all the secrets so that I could depart when the time came, with a scrubbed-out conscience."[6] The editor of a journal, *The Current Weekly* (Bombay, 1974), serialized the story and paid her handsome amounts of money, and though it hit the bookstalls in Kerala and in other parts of the country her relatives felt deeply embarrassed and perturbed over her revelations of certain well-guarded family secrets. What they specifically objected to was her confession of falling in love with so many men other than her own lawfully wedded husband. The natural outcome was that she was accorded no welcome on her return home, and that she was even ignored by her kith and kin. This necessitated her hurried return to the cosmoplitan city of Bombay. But she did not break her promise to the journalist and firmly stood her ground, completing the write-up of her autobiographical work on schedule. She felt immense pleasure in writing it, as she has disclosed in her Preface: "I have written several books in my life time, but none of them provided the pleasure the writing of *My Story* has given me."[7]

As an autobiography, *My Story* forcefully recounts Mrs. Das's life-story, spanning from her early childhood, through adulthood and youth, to the age of sickness and disease. It faithfully records her neglected early age in Calcutta, with her father lost in the business of selling Rolls Royces, Humbers and Bentleys — all imposing cars — to the Indian princes and their relatives and with her mother lying always on her belly on a large four-post bed, composing poems in Malayalam. Only the cook took care of her and her elder brother Mohandas in serving the meals and carrying them to a European school a furlong away. At school, they were humiliated and tortured by the white boys for their nut-brown skin. When a white dignitary visited the school, the dark boys and girls were whisked away to wait in the corridor behind the lavatories. The financial position of the Nalapat family (to which Kamala Das belonged) was precarious. Her parents were ill-matched to each other. They lived on the top floor of the repair-yard of the motor car company, where the father was employed, and the surroundings were none-too-happy and non-congenial. In collaboration with her brother, Kamala started a manuscript magazine. She was to write verses which made her cry, while he was to illustrate them. Once when they were on a picnic to the Victoria Gardens, she felt very lonely and slipped out to the old cemetery. Speaking of her mental condition at that time, she observes: "I was too young to know about ghosts. It was possible for me to love the dead as deeply as I loved the living."[8]

During the horrible days of the Second World War, the entire family was despatched to the ancestral home in Malabar, to the Nalapat House, precisely speaking. The house was spacious enough to lodge its seven inmates — Kamala's grand-mother, her aunt Ammini, her grand uncle (the poet), her great grandmother, her two sisters and Mahatmaji (*i.e.*, Mahatma Gandhi whose photo was hung in every room and whose presence was felt to be infectious). The members of the family wore *Khaddar* mostly. While Ammini was very attractive, her grand uncle Narayana Menon was a famous poet-philosopher. Her great grandmother's younger sister called Ammalu was a poetess devoted to Lord Krishna. In the meantime, Kamala had joined the Elementary School at Punnayurkulan and was infatuated with the charm of Govinda Kurup, an eighth-class boy treated as an outlaw by the class-teacher. The women of the best Nair families never mentioned sex, and Kamala remained innocent about it. The male Nairs were somewhat coarse and crude when their ire was aroused. They could then voluntarily change husbands for their daughters and nieces.

In one of his visits, Kamala's father found her to be turning rustic and uncultured, and so he shifted her to a boarding school run by the Roman Catholic nuns. She found some good companions there like Sarada Menon, Raji, Meenakshi, and the homely Annie (who got a handsome young lover). There her letters were censored, and she felt lonely and depressed. When she developed the red rash on her face and body, she was sent back home at Malabar. A sudden appearance of her father there brought her once again to Calcutta. The family had increased to six with the birth of a younger brother and a baby-sister. At this stage, Kamala wanted to marry a rich man to be a snob (p. 57). After attaining the age of puberty, she longed for a male child. A mysterious *Sanyasin* once came to her house, stayed there for a week or so, and then suddenly disappeared one fine morning, predicting the portending riots between the Hindus and the Muslims in 1947.

Thereafter, Kamala narrates the miserable tale of falling in love with her art-tutor, a Bengali fellow of 29, then with her English lady teacher — a lesbian affair, no doubt. The eighteen-year-old girl's behaviour towards Kamala while travelling in trains for two consecutive nights seems to be a curious mixture of fact and fiction, which is also to be witnessed in some other places in the autobiography. One day, a person working in the

Reserve Bank of India at Bombay came to her house; he was one Mr. Das, the would-be life-partner for her. But Mr. Das proved to be a mere bore with his crude sexual talks to her and his rude lustful advances towards her. What was more shocking to this sensitive girl of barely fifteen was his shameless description of "the sexual exploits he had shared with some of the maidservants in his house in Malabar" (p. 87). There was no softness, no tender love, no sweet words in him for her; he simply insisted upon her to bare her breasts and get her body bruised. All this bred a sense of loss and sadness in her. But for her there was no escape from him. Her parents and relatives had charted a course of life for her which was bound to be disastrous and miserable in the future. The marriage was solemnised against her wishes, and she could manage to remain a virgin for nearly a fortnight after it. Later she surrendered herself, became pregnant, and began vomiting and fell ill. She was sent back to Malabar, and a lovely little son was bom to her. When her husband came to Malabar, he spent most of his time with his cousins and sister-in-law, paying little or no heed to his weak wife. On his return to Bombay, the first letter that he wrote was not to Kamala but to a girl-cousin whom he had hugged feverishly. Now it became quite clear to Mrs. Das that he had married her for the sake of social status and financial gain, not for genuine love. So, she decided, "to be unfaithful to him, at least physically" (p. 99). She tried to entrap a young bricklayer busy in building a modem house for her father, but that did not come off. She then allowed one of her cousins to hold her in his warm arms for a few minutes and to kiss her on her mouth. Thereafter, her mother-in-law brought her to Bombay to resume her marital life. But since the mother-in-law felt quite uneasy there, all of them were again bundled out to Malabar. One night when she was all alone, the old Ayah allowed a drunken stranger to enter her room and commit an incomplete rape in the dark. After a few months, a second son named Priyadarsin was born to her. Returning to Bombay, her restlessness increased by leaps and bounds, and a skilled psychiatrist was summoned for her treatment. At the time of this nervous breakdown, a sort of physical intimacy developed between herself and her husband. She now surrendered herself totally to him in bed. After some time, she was sent to Malabar to be treated by an Ayurvedic physician. Her loved grandmother expired soon, and Kamala felt deeply disappointed over it, for "None had loved me as deeply as my grandmother" (p. 119). A week after her death, Mrs. Das fell in love with an extremely handsome young man while playing tennis at the Khar gymkhana. The young man sent a letter to her from Delhi, but that letter fell into the hand of her husband, who got annoyed with her. One day her pen-friend Carlo came personally to her in the autumn of her life. He pleaded with her to have free love, forgetting all about her grey-eyed gymkhana friend and about her indifferent husband. He wanted her to mn away with him, but being a mother of two children that was simply not possible for her.

In the meantime, Kamala's eldest son Monoo fell seriously ill, and she tended him properly. But her husband was ever lost in his files and the Co-operative Movement. To overcome their routined way of living, they proceeded on a picnic to Panchgani, a beautiful hill-station, where they felt greatly relaxed and rejuvenated. On returning from there, Mrs. Das fell seriously ill and bled almost to death. A sweet lady doctor was engaged to nurse her back to health, and she greatly succeeded in her mission.

Kamala's great grandmother who loved her deeply also passed away at this juncture. In Bombay, a Spanish made advances towards her, kissed her gently, and phoned her frequently. Meanwhile, her husband was transferred to Calcutta for a term of three years, and she did not like the cocktail parties of winter there: "It was from Calcutta that I lost my faith in the essential goodness of human beings" (p. 157). She became Carlo's Sita in Calcutta and floated in his robust white arms. Her husband was then sent to Delhi on three years' deputation, and here Kamala felt very young, very lovely and delightfully carefree (p. 171). She was presently pregnant for the third time, and was sent to Calicut to live with her parents during the period of delivery. A son was born to her again, and she christened him Jaisurya, but her husband loved to call him Shodoo. The new babe was looked after by a stout *sardarni* in the daytime.

Kamala's return to Delhi was marked by a sudden and serious breakdown of health. Her loved friend, Shirley, looked after her in the Willington Hospital. Mrs. Das was totally reduced, and looked like "a moulting bird" (p. 179). Even the well-known minister, Dr. V.K. Krishna Menon, came to her to enquire about her condition. Soon she recovered her health and yearned for human love. In her Man Nagar residence, she felt very happy, and here she had the good company of Prof. Thapar and Mrs. Luthra (the landlady). Like the phoenix, she rose from the ashes of her past and desired to have "an ideal lover" (p. 180). The pleasant, sunny winter of Delhi made her jubilant, but when she came to Bombay along with her transferred husband, she again felt lonely and sickly. More hectically she began to write stories and poems. Here at Churchgate she came into contact with a handsome dark man with a tattoo between his eyes. She fulfilled her lustful desires with him immediately after her serious sickness in Bombay. Her love-affairs with this elderly dark man were nothing short of adultery, as she confesses: "Like the majority of city-dwelling women, I too tried adultery for a short while, but I found it distasteful" (p. 193). Once again, she fell ill, and once again was admitted to the Bombay Hospital, and once again she recovered fully.

Lest Mrs. Das should create a bad name for herself, she hastens to add in chapter 44 that she was never 'a nymphomaniac' and that sex never interested her but at a certain loose moments. She granted sex to her husband to make him happy, otherwise he was a soul lost in his files and reports. He had aged prematurely, and she felt sorry for him. Sometimes he was abused and humiliated by his pigmy boss, and Mrs. Das advised him to resign the post immediately. She herself packed up at once and left for Malabar, where she reset the whole old estate in a new order. While living in the Nalapat House, she was loved and liked by all but the local wealthy, who often spread "lush scandals" about her way of life (p. 212). Her sudden heart attack and the measles of her two sons brought them back to Bombay, where she used to meet only her 'genuine friends.' She wrote a good deal at that time for her journals and readers. As a housewife, she was utterly useless, as she admits. Chapter 48 is patently wistful and fanciful. It is here that Kamala unravels her plans and dreams for the uplift of the poor and the downtrodden. She has a soft comer even for the builders and labourers, who participated in the musical evenings with all gaiety and optimism during the Ganesha festival in Bombay. Though she continues to be a heart-patient, she is not afraid to die, and *My Story* ends on a note of promise and envisions a bright future for children who will grow and prosper and who will "populate this earth" (p. 231).

As a piece of autobiography *My Story* is quite touching and revealing. It is written with utter honesty and openness. It does not conceal the scandalous facts and the physical lusts that Kamala Das felt for others. It is clear, she is dissatisfied with the love at the legitimate source and only in sickness she is truly attracted to her husband. As in her poetry, here too, there is a marked development in the matter of love — a marked transformation of physical plane of love into a divine or mystical plane of love. Time and again, she speaks of Lord Krishna, whom she regards as 'the ideal lover,' and repeatedly she pictures herself as his Radha, as his devoted votary. In one place, she remarks:

> Through the smoke of the incense
> I saw the beauteous smile of Krishna.
> Always, always, I shall love you I told him,

> ...only you will be my husband,
> Only your horoscope will match with mine.... (p. 96)

Her outspoken frankness in regard to love affairs has definitely given many a sleepless night to her family members and close relatives, but she prefers to die with a clean slate rather than with a sullied image. At places, Mrs. Das has also become a champion of woman's cause, a saviour of womankind. She speaks forcefully for the poor and the sufferers towards the close of her autobiography, and it is here that she adroitly mixes fact with fiction, naked reality with wistful thinking. When she talks of the city-dwellers and their seductive ways of life, she is quite convincing. She always commends medical practitioners and their sympathetic treatment of her during her illnesses, and remains loyal and devoted to her vocation of writing throughout. She tells us that she can write with a terrific speed — "nearly a thousand words a week" (p. 218), despite her ill-health and sagging spirits. *My Story* is the story of a liberalised woman who has discarded the burdensome travails of tradition and social taboos, who has had an eventless childhood and a diseased youth, and who has now matured and turned religious and spiritual in the last leg of her life. It is this unexpected change which has created flutter in the academic world rather than her fickle and fluid mood in going out of the way to please the men of her desires, sometimes even the old and the dark ones. Scholars have censured her for her "limits of over-exposure,"[9] and it is perhaps an awareness of their wrath that forced the autobiographer to change her attitude to life and literature as a whole.

There are striking similarities between Mrs. Das's autobiography and poetry. Both have an urgency of expression, a mood of confession, a lyrical effusion of powerful feelings. The latter part of the autobiography is littered with the poems of her choice which serve the purpose of epigraphs setting the tone and temper of a particular chapter in it. There are beautiful images, oratorical flashes, and monosyllabic expressions in both, and it is highly rewarding to make a comparative analysis of the two from this angle. For arresting images and analogies, one may quote the following excerpts from her *My Story*:

(i) There were no dark sewers running beneath the streets of his mind (p. 33).

(ii) I wanted like Sita to disappear into the bowels of the earth (p. 42).

(iii) In Bengal, the rain falls suddenly, with no warning, like the hysterical tears of a woman.... (p. 74).

(iv) Like alms looking for a begging bowl was my love which only sought for it a receptacle (p. 124).

(v) The books like a mother-cow licked the calf of my thought into shape and left me to lie at the altar of the world as a sacrificial gift" (p. 160).

These are merely random collections, and one can have many more such imagistic passages in Kamala's autobiography. The oratorical flashes are also to be had in her work, such as in the following:

> She made me laugh in disbelief. Was every married adult a clown in bed, a circus performer? (p. 72)

and again in:

> At night he was like a chieftain who collected the taxes due to him from his vassal, simply and without exhilaration (p. 98).

But her attitude towards her husband alters with the advancement of years. Later, she cares for his 'dignity' and looks upon him as the caretaker-head of the family. Thus, her attitude towards him remains ambivalent throughout, and her utterances may not be trusted like the oracle of Apollo. Reverting to her artistic excellences in the autobiography, we discover some fine flashes of 'poetic prose' in it. One may mark the following extracts in this connection:

(i) Each drew sustenance from the other's unspoken support (p. 51).

(ii) She had a mole on her cheek of which she spoke with great pride. It is a beauty spot, she said. Only one in million will get born with a beauty spot on the cheek.... (p. 56).

(iii) The Nepali tunes brought with them the mistiness of the mountains and their tragic loneliness (p. 146).

In them we have some catchy words and phrases, some nostalgic manifestations of natural beauty, some excellent monosyllabic utterances. The second extract is a remarkable illustration of a monosyllabic statement, full of lyrical impulse and accuracy of description.

It would be proper to close a study of *My Story* by drawing a close parallelism between it and her poetry. In theme and treatment, the two genres are seen doing the same task. Thus, in "The Dance of the Eunuchs," we find a graphic description of the dancing eunuchs:

> Their voices
> Were harsh, their songs melancholy; they sang of
> Lovers dying and of children left unborn...
> Some beat their drums; others beat their sorry breasts
> And wailed, and writhed in vacant ecstasy.[10]

And the same gripping scene has been colourfully painted by Mrs. Das in *My Story* thus: "And yet Calcutta gifted me with beautiful sights which built for me the sad poems that I used to write in my diary in those days. It was at Calcutta that I saw for the first time the eunuchs' dance." (p. 165). Such corresponding details lend credibility and reliability to her autobiography. Similarly, when she describes the sterile and uninspired love between herself and her husband in the poem "A Relationship":

> Betray me?
> Yes, he can, but never physically;
> Only with words that curl their limbs at
> Touch of air and die with metallic sighs.[11]

she simply states a harsh, naked truth bluntly. The same hurt feelings are articulated in her autobiography too on several occasions, such as in the following: "My husband thought that it [her special oil] had the sexiest scent of all. He was obsessed with sex. If it was not sex, it was the Co-operative Movement in India, and both these bored me" (pp. 134-35). Had Kamala been married to a poet, a writer, an artist, or an idealist-philosopher, it would have been a different story, presumably. But that was not to be, and hence with a faithful recordation of her life's trials and tribulations she has tried to lighten her burden, both mental and emotional. As hinted earlier, Kamala offers some interesting parallels in her poetry and autobiography when she comes to record her mystical experiences of Lord Krishna. In one of her poems titled "Radha," Kamala writes of herself thus:

> And virgin crying
> Everything in me
> Is melting, even the hardness at the core
> O Krishna, I am melting, melting, melting
> Nothing remains but
> You....[12]

and in another poem called "Ghanashyam," she forcefully asserts that Ghanashyam (another name of Lord Krishna) is her true lover and he occupies the whole of her heart:

> Ghanashyam,
> You have like a koel built your
> Nest in the arbour of my heart
> My life, until now a sleeping jungle
> Is at last astir with music.[13]

And such utterances are too many in the pages of *My Story*;[14] for example, the following one:

> Free from that last of human bondage, I turned to Krishna. I felt that the show had ended and the auditorium was empty. Then He came, not wearing a crown, not wearing make-up, but making a quiet entry. What is the role you are going to play, I asked Him. Your face seems familiar. I am not playing any role, I am myself, He said. In the old playhouse of my mind, in its echoing hollowness, His voice was sweet. He had come to claim me, ultimately. Thereafter he dwelt in my dreams. Often I sat crosslegged before a lamp reciting mantras in His praise.[15]

The same thought, the same tone, the same mystical emotion as witnessed in Kamala's verses overflows this prose passage. A kind of conversational tone is to be had in both, and there is a rare, purified atmosphere in them.

## II

*A Doll for the Child Prostitute* (1977) is a collection of Kamala's short stories, some of which were first published in such well-known magazines and periodicals as *Opinion, Quest, Debonair and Beautiful.* Put together, these stories combine to produce the picture of Mrs. Das as a forceful writer of gripping tales of innocence and eroticism. The blurb matter describes Kamala as "a sensitive and compelling author" of "engrossing stories."[16]

This beautiful, profound and captivating work begins with the title story, "A Doll for the Child Prostitute," which narrates the pitiable tale of a minor girl who should have been given a doll to play with rather than be raped by her own stepfather and later be forced into prostitution at the age of thirteen. The girl named Rukmani was sold to Ayee by her poor mother Anasuya. Ayee was a fat woman whose son had deserted her ten years ago and who always waited for his return home. The brothel she ran had seven immates (girls and women of diverse ages) in it, and she earned the support of Inspector Saheb (of Police Department) in managing her house. The Inspector was a man of loose moral character and demanded Rukmani to satisfy his lust. But Rukmani resisted his move by telling him — "I am not a whore."[17] When the Inspector Saheb visited her again, she started crying and rushed towards him calling him "Papa, papa" (p. 50). The Inspector assured her to protect her as his own grand-daughter who was then living with her parents at Nagpur. In the meantime, Mirathai (or Mira), another beautiful prostitute of the Ayee house, eloped with a college student, who was later arrested along with her by the Inspector

Saheb and his constables, who gave him a good thrashing. On the insistent appeal of Mira, Ayee went to the police chowki and got the boy freed.

Mira still loved the boy and wanted to go with him in order to live as wife and husband, but the boy kept mum. At this, Mira retorted furiously: "The ungrateful swine. He told me that he was twenty-four and that he had found a job at a mill. A liar. A stinking liar" (p. 55). Ayee allowed the boy go home, and Mira was retained in the brothel as a junior inmate, forfeiting her seniority to Saraswati, the most qualified of the lot. Suddenly, the postman brought a letter from Ayee's son and delivered it to her. The letter announced his arrival on the ensuing Saturday. Hearing the glad news, Ayee shared it with the Inspector Saheb, who advised her to marry Rukmani to her son. The long story brings out at least two most memorable and humane characters, and they are Ayee and the Inspector Saheb. Rukmani also gets a fair deal at the close of the story, but one feels that it comes a little late and hence can't redress her sufferings and indignities. The story is well within the range of Kamala's experiences, and it forcefully concentrates on one of the burning social problems of the day — corruption and prostitution rampant in India's metropolitan cities like Bombay.

The next story in *A Doll for the Child Prostitute* is "The Young Man with the Pitted Face," which is very slight in content and treatment. It tells a peculiar tale of a strange relationship between a dying woman and a healthy young man. The young man visited the ashen, blue woman in a hospital out of mere pity for her, but as soon as she recovered from her serious sickness he stopped coming to her despite her long wait and nocturnal vigil (p. 60).

Like the preceding story, "December" is also very thin in matter and execution. It seems to be a sentimental piece recounting the fulfilment in love of a man and a woman on a cold December day after she has recovered from a long illness. At the end of the story, the woman is heard saying so: "...I have become soft and sentimental, I shall never be able to write again, I am finished...."[18]

The story "A Little Kitten" highlights the inescapable predicament of a newly married woman who is settled in a small flat at Dadar. She gets bored throughout the day, as her husband serving in an insurance firm hardly has time to spend with her. She asks for a little kitten for her company, and in return the husband tickles her until she rolls over on the double-bed and is sexually assaulted. He mumbles to her thus: "I am your kitten, I am your little kitten."[19]

But with the passage of time, their loveful relationship suffers a setback and Miss Nadkar, his secretary, comes into the picture and creates doubts in the wife's mind. The wife is so upset that she does not care to adorn herself with a jasmine strand or colour her cheeks with a touch of rouge. One day, he comes dead drunk, and she tears her wedding saree into shreds. He proposes to her to visit her parents for a month, but she will go only when he accompanies her. He carries on his affairs with the beautiful secretary in some dark and dingy restaurants, though she is to be married off within four months. Returning home one day, he finds his wife, "so pink and healthy" (p. 67) and is greatly surprised. He rushes forward to embrace her, but seeing a long red scratch above her breasts, he recoils. He wants to know about the scratch, but she looks vacantly at the dusky sky. The subtle hint of the story writer seems to be towards the wife's intolerable agony which gets some relief in the intense embraces of some other man.

"Darjeeling" presents Raghavan, his wife and their four-year-old son. The wife is very fond of natural surroundings and snowcapped mountains of Darjeeling, but the husband has no time for such excursions. He is financially hard-pressed and can't afford to buy even a red silk saree for her on her birthday. She suddenly collapses on the floor with a sudden heart attack. The family-doctor is sent for, and he arranges her quick shift to the hospital. Her husband takes leave from the office and looks after the son. He is worried about the payment of the hospital bill. As he can't borrow money from anyone else, he writes an application for an overdraft of five hundred rupees. The young son reminds him at night that his mother "wants to see the snow" (p. 72).

The next story, "The Sign of the Lion," does not have any strong thread of narration. Once again, it highlights the passionate nature of man, who is a Brahmin husband coming in a red palanquin near midnight to lie beside his Nair wife. Like most of the stories in this collection, it is admittedly autobiographical. This is how Kamala depicts the man: "He clings to my breasts. He is my baby. People say that he will discard me. They say that he will take me to Lonavala and with tenderness kill me."[20] But the redeeming feature of the story is the expectancy of the wife, who will bear to him "a little lion" or "a beautiful lion-cub" (p. 76), though her man remains absent-minded when she breaks the news to him.

In "Sanatan Choudhuri's Wife," the faithlessness of Gopi Menon's wife is powerfully brought out. Evidently, Menon is a poor man, who can't afford to buy more than fifty Kanjivaram sarees for his wife. This fact coupled with her mumbling of the name of 'Sanatan' in her sleep arouses a strong suspicion in Menon that his wife is playing tricks with him. One day, he returns home early to test her fidelity, but to his utter amazement he finds her gone to the imposing house of Sanatan Choudhuri. He follows her closely, watches her going in and sharing a stylish breakfast with Sanatan. She even allows him to fondle her. When Menon gathers courage to question his wife and Sanatan, she simply replies, "Somebody has been trying to fool you...."[21] Rubbing his hands, Menon walks away to the nearest bus-stop.

The story "The Coroner" is slight in stuff and recounts the tragic death of Richie or Richard, the only son of Sylvester Louis Gomes, a collector of rents for his aged master. Richie aged 23 goes to the sea to bathe along with his pals and gets downed there. Gomes' master phones the Coroner to hand over the dead body of his son without any further inquests, and the Coroner whose grandfather had studied in England with the old master instantly obliges him. Gomes tells the story to one of his sympathetic rent-payers, a pregnant young lady of genial temper.

Next follows the story of a minor poet called Iqbal, who generally writes romantic and effervescent verses. As the story opens, Iqbal is confined to a hospital for consuming poison. Iqbal's room-mate of his YMCA days and his young, beautiful wife are there to take care of him in the hospital. Iqbal's verses have convinced the young woman that he is in deep love with a girl, but she does not know who this girl is. Her husband is always evasive on this point. Once or twice Iqbal comes to the young couple, on invitation of course, to take his Sunday lunches, but later he stops visiting them on one or the other pretext. In reality, Iqbal is a lover of this pretty, vivacious woman, and she too guesses it correctly. She says to Iqbal thus: "You are jealous of me...."[22]

"The Tattered Blanket" is a tender, pathetic tale of an old woman of eighty-five whose son Gopi is an official of the Government of India. Gopi comes home in Kerala from Delhi (where he is posted presently) to sell his share of property, but his widowed sister, Kamalam, does not like the idea. Gopi has already become indifferent to his ancestral house, even to the requirements of his old, ailing mother, who passes her cold nights in a tattered blanket and who demands "a new red blanket"[23] from him. The old mother is psychologically and compassionately portrayed herein. She is quite old, almost invalidated and mentally crippled. Her widowed daughter looks after her with all care and attention. A realistic picture of a white-collared, spendthrift Government officer is remarkably painted in this story.

Last of all comes "Leukaemia," which shows the fear-psychosis of a small girl in a boarding-house where she is sent by her insistent mother despite the wishes of her father. The mother wants her child to learn "discipline and the method of eating neatly with forks and knives."[24] The child though learnt a lot in these areas, she gets starved emotionally and dreams of her home and parents incessantly. The result is that she develops Leukaemia. When she is brought back home, her mother offers her plenty of toys to play with and informs her that she will not be sent back to the boarding-house again. At this, the child brightens up and feels immense relief.

## III

A thematic and structural survey of Kamala Das's prose convinces the reader that she writes it with the same urgency and the same feminine sensibility as she does her verses. Apparently, her immense popularity as a poetess has misguided her critics and reviewers who generally consider her poetry as the be-all and end-all of her artistic being. Even the doyen of IWE (Indian Writing in English), Prof. K.R. Srinivasa Iyengar seems to be satisfied by merely stating that "There is no doubt Kamala Das is a new phenomenon in Indo-Anglian poetry — a far cry indeed from Torn Dutt or even Sarojini Naidu."[25] It would be audacious to think of Devinder Kohli or Anisur Rehman while reviewing Kamala's prose writings. And hence her prose remains a virgin area to be explored and assessed afresh. Most of her prose works, like her verses, give the impression of having been written in great haste and with an urgency of purpose. Her words, phrases and expressions gush forth like a jet of water from a sprightly fountain, and in the rush of emotions and thoughts she sometimes loses track of syntax or proper sentence-structure, but her sincerity to 'the self is never shakable and her mastery of phrase and rhythm in her prose writings is simply superb and enviable. Kamala Das is unquestionably wedded to art, and her commitment to prose art allows the reader to forgive her for her minor blemishes of rash pronouncements, harsh judgments of males and their manners, aggressive feminism (mark, she has been nicknamed as 'femme fatale') and excessive physical or sexual exposures. In the golden realm of art, after all, nothing remains corruptible and contemptible, nothing sinful and lustful. This is well borne out by the mural paintings of Ajanta and Ellora and by the time-tested maxims of Vatsayan's Kāmasūtra.

## REFERENCES

1. Besides numerous articles and papers, three critical books on the poetry of *Kamala Das* have appeared so long — Devindra Kohli's Kamala Das (New Delhi: Arnold-Heinemann, 1975), Anisur Rahman's *Expressive Form in the Poetry of Kamala Das* (New Delhi: Abhinav Publications, 1981), and A.N. Dwivedi's *Kamala Das and Her Poetry* (Delhi: Doaba House, 1983). The third one is now being published by Atlantic Publishers, New Delhi.
2. Toru Dutt, "Our Casuarina Tree," *Ancient Ballads and Legends of Hindustan,* ed. A.N. Dwivedi, 2nd ed. (Bareilly: Prakash Book Depot, 1984), p. 182.
3. Thomas Gray, Elegy Written in a Country Churchyard," *The Oxford Book of English Verse*, ed. Sir Arthur Quiller-Couch (Oxford: At the Clarendon Press, 1953 ed.), p. 533.
4. One of them being the difficulty in getting her various essays and articles which were published in numerous magazines and journals.
5. Kamala Das, "Preface," *My Story*, Paperback ed. (New Delhi: Sterling Publishers, 1978), p. I. .
6. *Idem.*
7. *Idem.*
8. Kamala Das, *My Story*, p. 10.

   — All the textual quotations are absorbed in the body of the article itself hereafter.
9. Vimala Rao, "Kamala Das — The Limits of Over-Exposure," *Studies in Contemporary Indo-English Verse,* Vol. I, ed. A.N. Dwivedi (Bareilly: Prakash Book Depot, 1984), pp. 87-96.

   Miss Rao remarks here thus: "In life such self-exposure is suicidal, in art it is unpardonably boring" (p. 96).
10. Kamala Das, "The Dance of the Eunuchs," *Summer in Calcutta* (New Delhi: Everest Press, 1965), p. 9.
11. "A Relationship," Ibid., p. 18. The poem is found also in Kamala Das's *The Old Playhouse and Other Poems* (Madras: Orient Longman, 1973), p. 41.
12. *The Descendants* (Calcutta: Writers Workshop, 1967), p. 9.
13. Kamala Das, *Tonight, The Savage Rite* (New Delhi: Arnold-Heinemann, 1979), p. 18.
14. One may look up pp. 92, 95, 109, 113-14, 179, 190-91, 195, and 196-97 of her autobiography to substantiate the statement.
15. *My Story*, p. 195.
16. Kamala Das, *A Doll for the Child Prostitute* (New Delhi: India Paperbacks, 1977), the blurb.

17. *Ibid.*, p. 20.
18. "December," *A Doll for the Child Prostitute*, p. 63.
19. "A Little Kitten," *A Doll for the Child Prostitute*, p. 65.
20. "The Sign of the Lion," *A Doll for the Child Prostitute*, p. 76.
21. "Sanatan Choudhuri's Wife," *A Doll for the Child Prostitute*, p. 80.
22. "Iqbal," *A Doll for the Child Prostitute*, p. 92.
23. "The Tattered Blanket," *A Doll for the Child Prostitute*, p. 96.
24. "Leukaemia," *A Doll for the Child Prostitute*, p. 99.
25. K.R. Srinivasa Iyengar, *Indian Writing in English* (New Delhi: Sterling Publishers, 1984), p. 680.

# Select Bibliography


### (A) BOOKS BY KAMALA DAS

*Summer in Calcutta*. New Delhi: Everest Press, 1965. Published by Rajinder Paul.

*The Descendants*. Calcutta: Writers Workshop, 1967.

*The Old Playhouse and Other Poems*. Madras: Orient Longman Ltd., 1973.

*My Story*. New Delhi: Sterling Publishers Pvt. Ltd., 1976. It was first serialized in *The Current Weekly* of Bombay between January to December 1974.

*Alphabet of Lust*. New Delhi: Orient Paperbacks, 1976.

*A Doll for the Child Prostitute*. New Delhi: India Paperbacks, 1977.

*Tonight, This Savage Rite: The Love Poems of Kamala Das and Pritish Nandy*. New Delhi: Arnold-Heinemann (India) Pvt. Ltd., 1979.

### (B) HER ESSAYS and PROSE WRITINGS

"Obscenity and Literature," *Weekly Round Table* (April 23, 1972), pp. 31-32.

"Why Not More Than One Husband?" *Eve's Weekly*, XXVI, No. 19 (May 1972), p. 35.

"The Young Man with the Pitted Face," *Opinion* (August 31, 1973), p. 33.

"The She-Mouse Returns Home," *Imprint* (October 1973), p. 19.

"Frigidity and the Sepia-tainted Photograph," *Opinion* (Nov. 27, 1973), p. 30.

"I Studied All Men," *Love and Friendship*, ed. Khushwant Singh (New Delhi: Sterling Paperbacks, 1973), pp. 13-16.

"Only Those Above 55, Obsessed with Sex," *The Current Weekly* (Jan. 26, 1974), p. 22.

"The Gift of Roses," *The Indian P.E.N.*, 40, Nos. 4-5 (April-May 1974), pp. 11-12.

"I Have Lived Beautifully," *Debonair*, III, No. 5 (May 15, 1974), pp. 40-41.

"What Women Expect Out of Marriage and What They Get," *Femina* (July 5, 1974), pp. 20-21.

"Iqbal," *Debonair*, III, No. I (September 15, 1974), pp. 72-73.

"The Guest," *Modern Indian Short Stories: An Anthology* (New Delhi: Arnold-Heinemann, 1974), pp. 61-63.

"Sex: Mindless Surrender or Humming Fiesta?" *Femina* (June 6, 1975), p. 19.

"Leaves of Grass on the Kerala Coast," *Span*, XVI (October 1975), 30-31.

"Kalyani," *Quest* (March-April 1976), pp. 79-82.

"The Dispensary," *Enact*, 85-86, no page number given.

"The Sea Lounge," *Debonair* (1976), pp. 18-19.

"The Uninvited Poet," *Blitz* (February 5, 1977).

"Enough of a Pativarta," *Blitz* (April 9, 1977).

"The Invisible Poet," *Blitz* (April 30, 1977).

### (C) SECONDARY SOURCES

Bernard, John. Review of *Summer in Calcutta* in *The Journal of Commonwealth Literature*, 5 (July 1968), 117-18.

Daruwalla, K.N. *Two Decades of Indian Poetry*: 1960-1980. New Delhi: Vikas, 1980.

Deshpande, Gauri. "Foreword," *An Anthology of Indo-English Poetry*. New Delhi: Hind Pocket Books, no date.

De Souza, Eunice. "Kamala Das, Gauri Deshpande, Mamta Kalia," *Contemporary Indian Poetry in English*, ed. Saleem Peeradina. Bombay: Macmillan, 1972; rev. ed. 1977.

Dwivedi, A.N. *Indo-Anglian Poetry*. Allahabad: Kitab Mahal, 1979; second edition 1987.

—. Ed. *Indian Poetry in English*. New Delhi: Arnold-Heinemann, 1980.

Ezekiel, Nissim. "A Note on Kamala Das" in *Contemporary Poets of the English Language*, ed. Rosalie Murphy. London: St. James Press, 1970.

Gokak, V.K. Ed. *The Golden Treasury of Indo-Anglian Poetry*. New Delhi: Sahitya Akademi, 1970.

Gowda, H.H. Anniah. "Contemporary Indian Verse in English," *Indian Literature of the Past Fifty Years:* 1917-67. Mysore. Mysore University Press, 1970.

Hess, Linda. "Post-Independence Indian Poetry in English," *Quest*, 49 (April-June 1966), 37-38.

Iyengar, K.R.S. *Indian Writing in English.* Bombay: Asia Publishing House, 1962; 2nd ed. 1973.

Jaggi, Satya Dev. Review of *Summer in Calcutta* in Thought (April 16, 1966), 17-18.

Jussawalla, Adil. "The New Poetry," *Readings in Common-wealth Literature*, ed. William Walsh. Oxford: Clarendon, 1973.

Kohli, Devinder. *Virgin Whiteness: The Poetry of Kamala Das*. Calcutta: Writers Workshop, 1968.

—. *Kamala Das*. New Delhi: Arnold-Heinemann, 1975.

Kohli, Suresh. "The Poetic Craft of Kamala Das," *Thought* (March 16, 1968), 17-18.

. "A Direct Tone," Review of *The Descendants in Thought*, XX (Sept. 28, 1968), 16.

—. "Feminine Sensibility at Work: A Study of Some Indo-

English Women Poets," *Indian and Foreign Review* (March 1, 1971), pp. 19-20.

—. "Kamala Das," *Youth Times* (Sept. 6, 1974), pp. 37-41.

—. Review of *My Story* in Youth Times (Feb. 20-March 4, 1976), n.p.

Kulshrestha, Chirantan, *Contemporary Indian Poetry in English*. New Delhi: Arnold-Heinemann, 1980.

Lal, P. Ed. *Modern Indian Poetry in English*: An Anthology and a Credo. Calcutta: Writers Workshop, 1969.

McCutchion, David. "Must Indian Poetry in English Always Follow England," *Critical Essays on Indian Writing in English*, ed. M.K. Naik et al. Dharwar: Kamatak University Press, 1972.

Melwani, Murli Das. *Themes in Indo-Anglian Literature*. Bareilly: Prakash Book Depot, 1977.

Naik, M.K. "The Indianness of Indian Poetry in English," *Journal of Indian Writing in English*, 2, No. 1 (July 1973).

Nandy, Pritish. "Indian Poetry in English: The Dynamics of a New Sensibility," *Indian Literature* (March 1971), pp. 9-19.

—. "Introduction," *Indian Poetry in English Today.* New Delhi:

Sterling Publishers, 1973.

Narasimhaiah, C.D. *The Swan and the Eagle.* Simla: Indian Institute of Advanced Studies, 1969.

Padhi, Bibhu Prasad. "The Parallel Voice: A Study of the New English Poetry in India," *Quest*, 98 (Nov.-Dec. 1978), 39-46.

Parthasarathy, R. "Whoring after English Gods," *Perspectives*, ed. S.P. Bhagat. Bombay: Popular Prakashan, 1970.

—. Ed. *Ten Twentieth-Century Indian Poets.* New Delhi: O.U.P., 1977; 2nd ed. 1980.

Patel, Gieve. Review of *Summer in Calcutta* in Quest, 47 (Oct.-Dec. 1965), 103-104.

Peeradina, Saleem. Review of *A Doll for the Child Prostitute in Times Weekly* (June 19, 1977), p. 10.

Pillai, Mira. Review of *The Old Playhouse and Other Poems in The Indian P.E.N.* (Dec. 1973), pp. 19-21.

Pillai, Nita. Review of *Summer in Calcutta* in *Poetry India* (Jan.-March 1966), pp. 63-66.

Rahman, Anisur. *Expressive Form* in *the Poetry of Kamala Das.* New Delhi: Abhinav Publications, 1981.

Rao, Vepa. Review of *Alphabet of Lust in The Hindustan Times Weekly* (Sunday, July 17, 1977).

Rao, Vimala. "Kamala Das — The Limits of Over-Exposure," *Contemporary Indo-English Verse*, Vol. I, ed. A.N. Dwivedi. Bareilly: Prakash Book Depot, 1983, pp. 87-96.

Saha, Subhas C. "The Dance of Eunuchs," *Insights.* Calcutta: Writers Workshop, 1972.

—.Ed. *Modern Indo-Anglian Love Poetry.* Calcutta: Prayer Books, 1976.

Saradhi, K.P. "Three Indo-Anglian Women Poets: Gauri Deshpande, Roshen Alkazi and Kamala Das." *The Journal of Indian Writing in English* (Jan. 1974), pp. 33-35.

Sharma, M.L. "The Road to Brindavan: The Theme of Love in Kamala Das's Poetry," *Contemporary Indo-English Verse*, Vol. I, ed. A.N. Dwivedi, pp. 97-111.

——. *Kamala Das*. Patiala: Directorate of Correspondence Courses, Punjabi Univ., 1979.

Sinha, Krishna Nandan. Ed. *Indian Writing in English*. New Delhi: Heritage Publishers, 1979.

Siva Ramkrishna, M. "Contemporary Indian Poetry in English: An Approach," *Opinion*, 4, No. 1 (July 1974), 39-57.

Srinath, C.N. "Contemporary Indian Poetry in English," *The Literary Criterion* (Summer 1968), pp. 61-62.

Srivastava, Narsingh, "Some Indian Women Poets in English," *Indian Literature*, XVIII (1975), pp. 69-78.

Verghese, C. Paul. *Problems of Indian Creative Writers in English*. Bombay: Somaiya Publications, 1971.

—. *Essays on Indian Writing in English*. New Delhi: N.V. Publications, 1976.

Walsh, William. *Commonwealth Literature*. London: O.U.P., 1973.

Williams, H.M. *Indo-Anglian Literature*. Madras: Orient Longman Ltd., 1976.

# Index